Reading Power 系列

Advanced

★ 108課綱、全民英檢中／中高級適用

進階閱讀攻略

附翻譯與解析

簡薰育、唐慧莊　編著

Main Idea

Details

Infer

Critical Thinking

Vocabulary

三民書局

國家圖書館出版品預行編目資料

Advanced Reading：進階閱讀攻略／簡薰育,唐慧莊
編著.－－初版七刷.－－臺北市: 三民，2021
面；　公分.－－（Reading Power系列）

ISBN 978–957–14–5183–1　（平裝）
1. 英語 2. 問題集 3. 中等教育

524.38　　　　　　　　　　　98004828

 Reading Power 系列

Advanced Reading：進階閱讀攻略

編 著 者	簡薰育　唐慧莊
發 行 人	劉振強
出 版 者	三民書局股份有限公司
地　　址	臺北市復興北路 386 號 (復北門市) 臺北市重慶南路一段 61 號 (重南門市)
電　　話	(02)25006600
網　　址	三民網路書店 https://www.sanmin.com.tw
出版日期	初版一刷 2009 年 4 月 初版七刷 2021 年 9 月
書籍編號	S807360
I S B N	978-957-14-5183-1

三民書局

序

知識，就是希望；閱讀，就是力量。

在這個資訊爆炸的時代，應該如何選擇真正有用的資訊來吸收？
在考場如戰場的競爭壓力之下，應該如何儲備實力，漂亮地面對挑戰？
身為地球村的一分子，應該如何增進英語實力，與世界接軌？

學習英文的目的，就是要讓自己在這個資訊爆炸的時代之中，突破語言的藩籬，站在吸收新知的制高點之上，以閱讀獲得力量，以知識創造希望！

針對在英文閱讀中可能面對的挑戰，我們費心規劃 Reading Power 系列叢書，希望在學習英語的路上助你一臂之力，讓你輕鬆閱讀、快樂學習。

誠摯希望在學習英語的路上，這套 Reading Power 系列叢書將伴隨你找到閱讀的力量，發揮知識的光芒！

給讀者的話

　　英文閱讀測驗是許多高三同學的夢魘。以近年大考為例，閱讀測驗在考試中佔了不少比例。因此閱讀能力強，的確是英文科拿高分的重要關鍵。

　　閱讀測驗的題目通常不外乎下列五種：

㈠測驗文章的主旨大意 (Main Idea)

㈡測驗對於文章細節 (Details) 的理解

㈢測驗是否能推論 (Infer) 出字裡行間的引申意義

㈣判斷思考 (Critical Thinking) 文章的目的，作者的心態或是意見的呈現方式等

㈤測驗是否能從上下文當中來界定單字 (Vocabulary) 的意義。

　　本書即針對以上五大類題型所設計的閱讀測驗練習。文章的長度約在 350 字以下，單字範圍約在 Level 5～Level 6。本書取材範圍廣泛，舉凡歷史、文化、天文、地理、旅遊、環保、醫藥、衛生保健等等，均網羅其中。單字量涵蓋範圍雖大，文章卻並不深澀；其內容十分有趣，符合大考的出題範圍及類型。

　　閱讀英文文章時，最忌諱邊讀邊查字典。這樣的壞習慣，不但無法增進閱讀速度，還斷絕自己去培養猜測文意的能力 (guessing ability)。想想看：我們在讀中文報紙或小說時，會拿著字典查生字嗎？當然不會。我們都是邊讀邊思考猜測文意字義；讀的多，閱讀速度自

然增快，閱讀能力也因此增強。再說，考試時考生是不准用字典的。我常告訴學生：只要你勤快用功，閱讀量夠，重要的字句用語一定會常常出現在你眼前，想忘掉也不可能呢！做閱讀測驗練習的另一秘訣是：用碼錶測量自己的閱讀速度，並記下自己每篇所花費的時間。這個方法不但能增加專注力，還能時時反省檢測自己的閱讀狀況以及速度。日積月累地，閱讀能力必定增強。

　　本書附翻譯及詳細解析，建議讀者養成習慣每天做一篇或兩篇；做完後，再去核對解答；不要急著看翻譯，先找出自己答錯的原因，再去查字典以理解其中的關鍵字句。五十篇做完，相信你下次考試時，必能得心應手。

　　最後，感謝三民書局編輯部同仁鼎力協助本書付梓，也期盼因此帶給讀者更多心靈上的滋潤。

Acknowledgements:

The articles in this publication are adapted from the works by:
Betty Carlson
Carol Sonenklar
Charles Olmsted
Douglas Hinnant
Editage
Fariba Mitchell
Helen Johnson
Ian Fletcher
James Baron
Jason Grenier
Jennifer Heuson
Justin Silves
Karen LeVasseur
Lee Fernon
M. J. McAteer
Matthew Wilson
Ming Wong
Monideepa Banerjee
Paul Geraghty
Paul Hsiung Go
Quinn Genzel
Rashimi Kalia
Rhishipal Ramachandran
Stephen Goodchild
Sue Farley
Tara Benwell
Theodore J. Pigott

Table of Contents

Unit 01 The Changing World of English   2

Unit 02 Our Furry Friends   4

Unit 03 A Quick Glimpse of Rotorua   6

Unit 04 Sound Effects   8

Unit 05 Stuck on Glues   10

Unit 06 The Big Problem   12

Unit 07 The City Life and the Country Life   14

Unit 08 The Most Daring Writer and The Most Darling Child   16

Unit 09 Being All Heart   18

Unit 10 The Camera: the Star of Shooting   20

Unit 11 The Tilted Tower   22

Unit 12 Death-defying Daring   24

Unit 13 Keep It Real!   26

Unit 14 The Leverage   28

Unit 15 Tourist Destination in Danger   30

Unit 16 The Hottest Sports on Ice   32

Unit 17 The Small Giant   34

Unit 18 Less Boo, More Boost   36

Unit 19 Toilet Tale   38

Unit 20 Terminal Tuberculosis Thrives   40

Unit 21 Pros and Cons   42

Unit 22 Venice: Sinister Serenissima   44

Unit 23 The Eiffel Tower: A Daredevil's Dream   46

Unit 24 Give Them a Dog Chance   48

Unit 25 As Blind As a Bat   50

Unit 26 Smells Like True Love   52

Unit 27 Another Inconvenient Truth 54

Unit 28 The Powerless Poseidon 56

Unit 29 Puppy Poop Preparation 58

Unit 30 The Sky's the Limit 60

Unit 31 A Sign of No More Sighs 62

Unit 32 Enter the "Ethical" Market 64

Unit 33 Our X-files: Xaggerated and Xtraordinary 66

Unit 34 Selling and Smelling 68

Unit 35 The Mega Monolith 70

Unit 36 The Successful Sales Program 72

Unit 37 A Shot for Clot 74

Unit 38 Grow a Gift for Gift Giving 76

Unit 39 Let's Dive In! 78

Unit 40 Thought-provoking Tragedies 80

Unit 41 All Aboard the Orient Express 82

Unit 42 Our Misunderstood Mate 84

Unit 43 Distraction for Drivers 86

Unit 44 Beavers Bite 88

Unit 45 Sea Fans, Seeking Defense 90

Unit 46 Get the Adrenaline Going 92

Unit 47 Giant Squid Finally Sees the Light 94

Unit 48 The High-flying Job 96

Unit 49 The Bold Charlie Brown 98

Unit 50 Sweat and Sweet 100

Answer Key 103

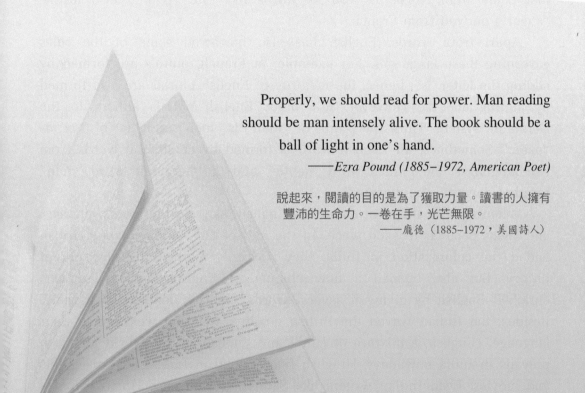

Properly, we should read for power. Man reading should be man intensely alive. The book should be a ball of light in one's hand.

——*Ezra Pound (1885–1972, American Poet)*

說起來，閱讀的目的是為了獲取力量。讀書的人擁有豐沛的生命力。一卷在手，光芒無限。

——龐德（1885–1972，美國詩人）

ADVANCED READING 2

UNIT 01

The Changing World of English

English has descended from the language spoken by Germanic invaders like the Saxons and the Angles. The Angles spoke "Englisc," and it is from this word that the word "English" itself is derived. Over time, new words were coined from the languages of other invaders like the Norse and the French. Thus, English contains words like "anger" that come from Norse as well as words like "ire" (which also means "anger") derived from French.

Apart from words, English has also borrowed some of the rules governing these languages. For example, in French, plurals are formed by adding the letter "s"; hence, the majority of English plurals are also formed by adding an "s." However, few other English plurals adhere to the Germanic system. Thus, the plural of "man" is "men" and that of "ox" is "oxen." Sometimes, an English word is formed by combining words from two languages: the French word "gentle" and the Germanic word "man" together generate "gentleman"!

When used in different countries, English takes on the words, phrases, and styles peculiar to each place. In the mid of 20th century, when British ended the colonization in India, they not only marked the new era of history, but also opened a new chapter of English. Indian language enriched English by giving it several words such as "loot" and "bazaar." Besides, the Indian waved the British goodbye but said welcome to their language. Hinglish, a mixture of Hindi and English, is the hybrid language prevails in India nowadays. Hinglish figures high in Indian advertisements and movies. Even Indian writers like Salman Rushdie use Hinglish in his novels. Today, Indian English has a rhythmic tone of speaking due to the influence of various Indian languages with their natural rhythm.

Some linguists consider Hinglish and similar phenomena bad English, but others like the philosopher Ivan Illich believe that "language would be totally callous if it were totally taught." Although English has changed through contact with other languages, its origins are still Germanic.

_____ 1. This passage mainly discusses _____ .
   (A) the major origins of the English language
   (B) the influences of other languages on English
   (C) the impact of the English language
   (D) the importance of the English language

_____ 2. The word "English" originated from _____ .
   (A) German
   (B) French
   (C) the Saxons
   (D) the Angles

_____ 3. Which of the following about the development of English is true?
   (A) The plural "oxen" follows the rule of French rules.
   (B) "Ire" is the word borrowed from Hindi.
   (C) Indians blended Hindi with English and created their own language.
   (D) The origins of English are from the Saxons and the Angles.

_____ 4. According to the passage, which of the following is NOT true?
   (A) Hinglish is widely used in Indian media.
   (B) The rules of forming plurals in English are all derived from French.
   (C) The word "loot" is borrowed from Indian language.
   (D) Some linguists don't agree with the foreign impacts on English.

_____ 5. What does hybrid mean in the passage?
   (A) Mixed.
   (B) Respectful.
   (C) Extinct.
   (D) Complicated.

Time and industry produce every day new knowledge.   時間與勤勞，使學識與日俱增。

Our Furry Friends

Polar bears live in the Arctic—a forbidding land of ice and snow, where few creatures can survive. Polar bears don't hibernate; they stay active all year round, even spending a lot of time in the icy water. How do they do it? The answer lies in that enormous white fur coat and the special skin beneath it.

White fur allows polar bears to blend in with the snowy surroundings in the far north. The largest land predators disguise themselves to sneak up on their prey. It also provides camouflage when the bears find themselves being hunted. But in fact, the coat mainly acts as the first line of defense against the elements.

The outer layer of a polar bear's coat is made up of hair shafts. The shafts are hollow and transparent, and look a lot like thin drinking straws. They reflect sunlight, making the coat look white. Being hollow allows air to stay trapped inside them, which provides much needed insulation. Another important thing about the hair shafts is that they do not get matted. This allows the bear to shake off water, snow, and ice from its coat easily. As a second line of defense, the bear has a thick, woolly undercoat of fur beneath this outer layer of hair shafts. This provides it with even more warmth.

Underneath all that white fur, a polar bear's skin is actually black, which helps absorb the warmth from the sunlight and hold it in, instead of reflecting it away. Like whales and seals, polar bears also have a thick layer of fat called blubber under their skin. Blubber provides even more insulation.

All animals have to adapt to their environment, and polar bears face an especially tough challenge. Only the strong survive in the Arctic. But with a white fur coat, black skin, and a layer of blubber, polar bears are able to make this desolate place their home.

_____ 1. Based on this passage, which statement best describes polar bears?

   (A) The survival of the fittest.

   (B) Appearances are deceptive.

   (C) Extinction is around the corner.

   (D) Animal instincts are inborn.

_____ 2. Which of the following is NOT a way to keep polar bears warm?

   (A) They sleep through the winter to preserve energy.

   (B) Their white fur can stop cold from entering and keep heat inside.

   (C) They have black skin to absorb warmth from the sunlight.

   (D) The thick layer of fat stored under their skin can hold warmth.

_____ 3. Polar bears can easily shake off water, snow, and ice from their fur because their fur _____ .

   (A) is thick and insulated

   (B) is hollow and transparent

   (C) matches the surroundings

   (D) won't get stuck together in a mass

_____ 4. The passage suggests that _____ .

   (A) polar bears are the only animal in the Arctic

   (B) all bears except polar bears hibernate

   (C) polar bears' fur is not actually white

   (D) polar bears often fall prey to seals and whales

_____ 5. As used in this passage, **camouflage** refers to a way _____ .

   (A) to leave polar bears under attack

   (B) to make polar bears difficult to spot

   (C) to help polar bears find enough food

   (D) to enable polar bears to adapt to the environment

A Quick Glimpse of Rotorua

From the moment you enter this quiet little town you know you are somewhere quite different. Smoky threads of steam rise from everywhere—be it a park, street or behind buildings—clouding the deep blue sky in misty grey. Strong rotten scent of sulfur floats through the air that otherwise smells of fresh morning dew. Geysers of steaming water roar from the ground while pools of mud bubble on and on. Rotorua, a town in North Island of New Zealand, carries the legacy of nature's anger on her humble shoulders.

The town is the cradle of Maori culture. In Maori language "roto" means lake and "rua" is two, as it was the second major lake that the Maori Chief, Ihengahe, discovered when he arrived with his people in the 14th century.

An experience not to be missed is the daily eruption of Lady Knox Geyser. Every day from ten thirty a.m., fountains of hot water shoot up from the tip of a small grey mound for about an hour. It is the lifesaver of the region. It provides an outlet for the coiled up pressure inside the earth that otherwise may turn fatal any moment. The tourism bureau has cleverly controlled the eruption to make it the most popular tourist attraction. It is a mere trick of science. By adding salt in the opening, the surface tension is lowered and water comes out.

The other main region is the Waimangu Volcanic Valley. It bears a sad note. In 1886, the Mt. Tarawera exploded, showering the entire countryside in red-hot lava, rocks and ash. In no time, the surrounding villages were buried under debris that killed everything. Years later the site was dug out. The places—markets, schools, and restaurants—look like they were in the middle of a busy day when the villagers suddenly decided to do the magician's vanishing act.

In Rotorua, you feel the strength of nature's emotions. Unable to control her anger, nature does bring in misery and unhappiness onto the earth from time to time. But the beautiful location formed out of it also shows her love and concerns.

_____ 1. The passage mainly focuses on the _____ .
   (A) colorful scenery of Waimangu Valley
   (B) scenery and the history of Rotorua
   (C) destruction of an old town
   (D) strength of nature's emotions

_____ 2. Rotorua is unusual in that _____ .
   (A) it is the cradle of Maori culture
   (B) it shows nature's humbleness
   (C) it bears a sad note
   (D) it has many hot springs

_____ 3. Which of the following statements is NOT true?
   (A) Tourists seldom go to Waimangu Volcanic Valley for fear of the sudden eruption there.
   (B) Tourists can feel the strength of Nature's emotions in Rotorua.
   (C) Rotorua is an ideal place for health resorts.
   (D) The daily eruption of Lady Knox Geyser reduces the chances of volcanic eruption.

_____ 4. The eruption of Mt. Tarawera presents the fact that _____ .
   (A) nature shows her love and concerns all the time
   (B) nature could kill everything in a moment
   (C) all the villagers hated Mt. Tarawera
   (D) Maori's culture has existed for centuries

_____ 5. What does **the magician** refer to in the passage?
   (A) Tourists.
   (B) Scientists.
   (C) Mother Nature.
   (D) the Maori Chief, Ihengahe.

We can learn something new any time we believe we can.
只要相信可以，我們隨時都能夠學習新事物。

UNIT 04

Sound Effects

Back in the mid-1980's, everyone in the world suddenly became American. They were either singing along with or tapping their feet to the voice blaring from many radio speakers. The voice sang "I was born in the U.S.A. I was born in the U.S.A.," over and over. With that song, the album with the same title, and a worn but defiant voice, Bruce Springsteen had arrived.

Born in the U.S.A had seven hit singles and sold 10 million copies worldwide. It made the New-Jersey-born rock singer and songwriter an icon. Yet for all his enduring popularity, Springsteen has been largely misunderstood. Springsteen was quickly cast as the symbol of U.S. arrogance. Many pump-fisted to "Born in the U.S.A.," and numerous others considered the song's anthem-like beat and lyrics too American, too cocky. But anyone who listens carefully to the lyrics of the song would know better. In the song, Springsteen describes a man who's "ten years burning down the road/Nowhere to run ain't got nowhere to go." He does not glorify America, but offers social criticism about it.

Since the 1970's, Springsteen has been singing about ordinary people's dreams, their fulfillment and their shattering life experience. Factory workers, clerks, the disadvantaged—these were the people Springsteen gave voice to. He offered small-town teenagers hope in "Born to Run": "We gotta get out while we're young/'Cause tramps like us, baby we were born to run"; he sang of the plight of American blue-collar immigrants in "The Ghost of Tom Joad"; and he wrote about AIDS in "Streets of Philadelphia." For decades now, Springsteen has chronicled the lives of Americans who normally do not have their stories told. His description of America—as a land of dreams and defeat—has earned him global fans who shared the same hopes and miseries as his songs' characters. Springsteen has not slowed down now that he is in his early sixties. In *The Rising*, his best-selling album mostly about average lives changed and lost after 911, Springsteen sings, "May the living let us in, before the dead tear us apart." Let's hope the world keeps listening.

_____ 1. The writer proves that Springsteen is misunderstood by _____.
   (A) citing part of his lyrics
   (B) quoting a paragraph from his autobiography
   (C) interviewing his closest friend
   (D) presenting exact statistics

_____ 2. The passage suggests that Springsteen wrote "Born in the U.S.A" to _____.
   (A) glorify America as a land of dreams
   (B) pass judgments about social problems in America
   (C) integrate different ethnic groups into the melting pot
   (D) dispel people's misunderstanding over his patriotism

_____ 3. Which of the following songs by Springsteen voices the hardships of American blue-collar immigrants?
   (A) "Born in the U.S.A."
   (B) "Born to Run."
   (C) "The Ghost of Tom Joad."
   (D) "Streets of Philadelphia."

_____ 4. Springsteen's enduring popularity lies in the fact that _____.
   (A) his voice is worn but defiant
   (B) he is matured by his life experiences
   (C) ordinary people can identify with the characters in his songs
   (D) he encourages people to tell him about the struggle in their daily lives

_____ 5. The word **cocky** in the passage can be best replaced by _____.
   (A) rhythmic
   (B) aggressive
   (C) passionate
   (D) arrogant

Reading makes a full man, meditation a profound man, discourse a clear man.
閱讀讓人充實，思考讓人沉著，交談讓人清明。

UNIT 05

Stuck on Glues

Glues are perhaps the longest used artificial substance by man. In fact, the development of glues has kept pace with human development.

The Babylonians were perhaps the first to use glue as an **adhesive** material. Their broken vessels were repaired using animal glue. Records indicate that ancient Egyptians used glue for making furniture about 4,000 years ago. They used hide glue obtained from the hides and skins of animals. Hide glue was considered a major discovery until the Romans and Greeks used fish glue for bonding together thin pieces of wood. Woodwork needed stronger glues, and this led to the development of fish glue.

Even though glue technology was much evolved in many countries and early civilizations, many of their combinations are still unknown to us. For example, the glue developed and used by Genghis Khan and his army was well known for its binding properties, but nobody knows the secret combination that he used to make it. During the middle ages, glues were used for making furniture and musical instruments as well as in architecture, fishing and war.

Industrial production of glue started in Holland around 1750, and it is the first country to have had a commercial glue factory. Britain was the first country that awarded a patent for a type of fish glue. During the early 19th century, glues were made from bones, rubber, synthetic materials, petroleum products, etc. The Industrial Revolution and the World Wars hastened the development of glue technology and soon glues were made from synthetic compounds such as phenolic resins. Modern technology has mostly done away with glues made from animal by-products. Chemical glues are durable, have better binding capacities, and withstand extremes of temperature and pressure. Today, most of the old-world glues have been replaced with synthetic compounds.

Interestingly, glues were available 6,000 years ago although significant development and research on them happened only during the last 100 years. Glues have become an inevitable necessity in the lives of humans.

_____ 1. The passage mainly deals with _____ .
    (A) the purposes of using glues
    (B) the inventors of glues
    (C) special types of glues
    (D) the history of glues

_____ 2. Before Roman times, people used _____ glues.
    (A) fish
    (B) hide
    (C) secret
    (D) synthetic

_____ 3. According to the passage, glues were used _____ years ago.
    (A) 6,000
    (B) 100
    (C) 5,000
    (D) 1,000

_____ 4. Which of the following is NOT true?
    (A) Genghis Khan once developed secret glue.
    (B) Britain had the first glue factory in history.
    (C) In modern days, people use synthetic glues.
    (D) World Wars promoted the development of glues.

_____ 5. In the passage, **adhesive** means _____ .
    (A) loose
    (B) strong
    (C) sticky
    (D) synthetic

Use a book as a bee does flowers.　讀書如蜜蜂採花，吸取其中精華。

The Big Problem

From the 18th century onward, the world has probably never known a greater, keener satirist than Irish writer Jonathan Swift. In his famous *Gulliver's Travels*, Swift criticized and tried to educate the human race. He wanted people to realize their flaws and get rid of them. How **appalled** Swift might be, were he alive today: things have not changed much in the last 200 years.

In his story Swift creates a race of giants called the Brobdingnagians. Everything about them and their society was huge. The pores of their skin, their excrement and the insects that bothered them were so large and disgusting. Since Gulliver was so much smaller than the Brobdingnagians, he was forced to focus on the "little" things they ignored. Swift therefore used these giants to comment on his society's habit of avoiding the seemingly trivial, unpleasant but important things in life. Sadly, we are still a race who neglects the undesirable while noteworthy occurrences in our world.

The media and we who patronize them regularly ignore news much bigger than current headlines. For example, a celebrity once dominated the airwaves because of the child abuse charges against him. But hardly anything is said about the humanitarian tragedy in Uganda, where rebel forces are forcing people into starvation. We were also like Brobdingnagians when the coverage of Iraq war was bigger than that of the earthquake which killed 15,000 people in Iran—a number the war in Iraq cannot, thankfully, match. And the list can go on and on. We had swept under the rug of our consciousness the famine in North Korea, the massacre in Rwanda, and the zillion of AIDS victims in Africa. It is natural for us to shorten our focus on awful news reports because they are too horrible to think about or too far away from where we are; yet if we do not pay attention to terrible calamities, how can we help people in dire need? Millions are counting on us to have a fair and accurate sense of what is small or big. For them all, we should stop being Brobdingnagians.

_____ 1. The purpose of this passage is mainly to _____.
  (A) praise Jonathan Swift as a satirist
  (B) criticize the British society of the 18th century
  (C) reveal the tragedies and calamities of the present world
  (D) remind people to pay attention to what is really important in life

_____ 2. Which of the following statements about *Gulliver's Travels* is true?
  (A) The stories are based on Swift's personal adventure and experience.
  (B) The Brobdingnagians are miniature human beings.
  (C) The insects that bothered Brobdingnagians are not the normal size.
  (D) Gulliver is so tiny that the Brobdingnagians even neglect his existence.

_____ 3. According to the passage, the number of deaths in the Iraq war is
  _____.
  (A) up to 15,000
  (B) under 15,000
  (C) over 15,000
  (D) equal to 15,000

_____ 4. The passage implies that _____.
  (A) humans are still as bloodthirsty as they used to be
  (B) the media is only interested in scandals of celebrities
  (C) people tend to be blind to miseries far away from them
  (D) we should focus on terrible occurrences caused by human faults rather
      than on natural disasters

_____ 5. In the passage, the word **appalled** means _____.
  (A) shocked
  (B) content
  (C) relieved
  (D) pleased

Reading is to the mind what exercise is to the body.　讀書頤神養性，運動強健體魄。

UNIT 07

The City Life and the Country Life

Cities are big crowded places full of noises and pollution. Its hectic lifestyle can slowly run down people's spirits and energy. City people are so wrapped up in their own lives and schedules that they hardly interact with their fellow citizens. They may feel awfully lonely, though surrounded by a slew of people and diversions. Therefore, many city residents caught up in the rat race often dream of simpler, more relaxing lives in the country.

Those who move to the country need to make major adjustments to their lives. Cities, while confusing, also offer choices and conveniences. No longer does one have a variety of restaurants or stores to choose from. There may only be one or a few small places to buy food, and visiting a 7–11 shop can be up to a 30-minute ride away. Also, nearly all transport must be done by car, instead of the options of bus, subway or maybe ferry in most cities. In order to conduct such official or government business as driver's license registration, voter registration, etc., one must still return to a city, or at least a larger town.

However, in exchange for this lost convenience in country life, much is gained in return. The air and water are definitely cleaner; the traffic, if any, is much lighter, and parking is absolutely no longer a problem. People in general are much more relaxed and friendly, and children have a much freer, safer and more peaceful environment to grow up in. Older people tend to have a greater attachment to family, friends, and location in small towns than in anonymous and self-absorbed cities.

Changing from a crowded, frantic environment to an open and relaxing one may be easy. But changing from a busy, self-centered, and materialistic life to a slower and more community-oriented one may be much more difficult. Most are unable to make such a transition and return soon to the excitement, convenience, and security of their city routine. Some, though, are able to make the change, to the benefit of themselves and their families. These few have indeed made their dreams into reality.

_____ 1. What does the passage mainly deal with?

(A) City people cannot endure their busy lives in the city.

(B) City people cannot endure the boring life in the country.

(C) It is difficult for city people to adjust themselves to the country life.

(D) It is necessary for city people to move to the country.

_____ 2. The writer indicates that city people _____ .

(A) tend to isolate themselves

(B) are used to the crowded environment

(C) live better lives

(D) don't know how to relax themselves

_____ 3. According to the passage, the best advantage of city life is _____ .

(A) a busy, self-centered life style

(B) clean air and light traffic

(C) a safer, peaceful environment

(D) conveniences and transportation

_____ 4. We can infer from the passage that _____ .

(A) not many country people like to live in the city

(B) not many city people can endure simple, slow-paced country life

(C) city people can make more adaptation to their environment

(D) country people enjoy more fun than city people

_____ 5. In the passage, **rat race** refers to _____ .

(A) people running around aimlessly

(B) people running after rats anxiously

(C) rats competing with one another

(D) rats searching for food

An investment in knowledge always pays the best interest.
知識上的投資，永遠有最好的報酬。

The Most Daring Writer and the Most Darling Child

In 1885, Mark Twain's novel *The Adventures of Huckleberry Finn* was first published. It tells the story of a rebellious teenager who travels down the Mississippi river on a raft with a runaway slave called Jim. The book turned Twain into a household name and is now regarded as a typically American work of art. The great American novelist Ernest Hemingway remarked: "All modern American literature comes from one book by Mark Twain called *Huckleberry Finn*." What made *Huckleberry Finn* such a uniquely American novel?

One important factor is Twain's employment of American slang and idiom. Before Twain, few American authors had used distinctly American speech in their writing. Most of them imitated the elegant dialog of British authors, for great literature was not supposed to contain the coarse language of common people. However, Twain wanted readers to be able to identify with his characters and their manners of speaking. Huckleberry, the story's narrator, is uneducated and speaks ungrammatical English. When, for instance, he relates a tale of a woman teaching him about the Bible, he says: "she learned me," instead of "she taught me." He also uses slang words like "ain't" in place of "am not," "isn't," and "aren't" a lot. Jim's African-American dialect is also full of slang. Readers today can sometimes find Jim's dialog difficult to grasp.

Another thing that gives the novel a specifically American flavor is the theme of freedom. Jim wants to escape from his life as a slave and Huck tries to help him. At first Huck is not sure whether he is doing the right thing but when Jim becomes his friend, he is certain about it. It is clear that Twain meant to expose racist attitudes and the injustice of slavery. The novel also deals with another kind of freedom, which is the freedom to roam. Huck is free from society's rules as he floats along the Mississippi, with no particular destination in mind. This idea of freedom was to influence later American literary works.

_____ 1. This passage is primarily about _____.
   (A) why *The Adventures of Huckleberry Finn* is a successful novel
   (B) how *The Adventures of Huckleberry Finn* influences the modern American literature
   (C) Mark Twain's status in the 19th century American literature
   (D) a profile of the American society of the early 19th century

_____ 2. Mark Twain wrote *The Adventures of Huckleberry Finn* in order to _____.
   (A) justify racism and anti-social attitudes
   (B) admire the friendship between Huckleberry and Jim
   (C) introduce the language of common American people
   (D) expose the injustice of slavery and honor the value of freedom

_____ 3. For modern readers, what makes the dialog of Mark Twain's characters difficult to understand?
   (A) It is too elegant.
   (B) It is full of slang words.
   (C) It is full of metaphors and similes.
   (D) It follows British English grammar rules.

_____ 4. We can infer from the passage that _____.
   (A) Mark Twain was in favor of racism and slavery
   (B) Mark Twain and Ernest Hemingway were contemporary writers
   (C) Huck and Jim's navigation down the Mississippi river was smooth
   (D) *The Adventures of Huckleberry Finn* may not have been regarded as a great literary work in Mark Twain's day

_____ 5. The word **coarse** in this passage is closest in meaning to _____.
   (A) sensible
   (B) fluent
   (C) vulgar
   (D) technical

That is a good book which is opened with expectation and closed in profit.
開卷時引人入勝，掩卷時使人獲益—這就是好書。

UNIT 09

Being All Heart

The news should not have surprised her. Everyone in the country knew it was going to happen. But it was shocking: they had killed her husband.

Corazon Aquino (whose name means "heart" in Spanish) had been married to Benigno for 29 years when he was murdered in 1983. He was the number one political enemy of Philippine dictator Ferdinand Marcos. Benigno, for years, had called for democracy and freedom in his country; for that, he and his family were exiled to the United States. Though people warned him that Marcos would get rid of him once he returned to his native country, he persisted. His death instantly made him a martyr, and propelled Corazon into the role of leader of a revolution.

A simple housewife, Corazon had no desire to be a political hero. But she knew the oppressed people needed her, and the Philippines needed change. Her heart could not help but respond to her compatriots' demand for fairness. Corazon then ran for presidency against Marcos. Though Marcos was announced the winner, it was obvious to everyone that Corazon got most of the votes. The elections were rigged. Thousands of people, if not millions, poured into the streets protesting for days. Marcos, realizing his defeat, left the Philippines, never to return. A successful and peaceful "People Power" revolution had taken place. Had it not been for Corazon's decision to accept leadership, it never would have happened.

As the new president, Corazon kept her integrity and sought changes where they were most necessary. She restored the country's freedom of the press, changed the constitution so tyrants like Marcos could never rise to power again, and ensured peace in the country's troubled south. Above all, she gave Filipinos hope that an ordinary person could rule a country with decency, honesty, and a sense of justice. Up to now, whenever she appears in public as a retired politician, her shining charisma would make people shout her nickname, "Cory! Cory!" Undoubtedly, Corazon Aquino is all heart.

_____ 1. What is this passage mainly about?

    (A) The current political situation in Philippine.

    (B) The autobiography of a retired female politician.

    (C) How Philippine became a democratic country.

    (D) How Corazon Aquino became the president of Philippine.

_____ 2. Corazon ran for presidency because _____.

    (A) she wanted to take revenge on her rivals

    (B) she wanted to prove her ability in politics

    (C) her country was in desperate situations and needed reforms

    (D) her husband was murdered and she wanted to find out the murderer

_____ 3. According to the passage, the result of the election between Corazon and Marcos was _____.

    (A) fair

    (B) unfair

    (C) exciting

    (D) amazing

_____ 4. Which of the following is true?

    (A) Marcos was exiled to the States after his failure in the election.

    (B) Marcos led "People Power" revolution, and he failed.

    (C) Corazon changed the constitution so that Marcos couldn't be president again.

    (D) Corazon controlled the media to her own advantage.

_____ 5. What does **martyr** mean in the passage?

    (A) A sufferer for a cause.

    (B) A victim of a disaster.

    (C) A shameless liar.

    (D) A hateful devil.

There is more treasure in books than in all the pirate's loot on Treasure Island.
金銀島上海盜的金山銀山，比不上書中的黃金屋。

UNIT 10

The Camera: the Star of Shooting

It all began in 1839, when Sir John F. W. Herschel first used the word "photography" to explain his experiments to capture an image of the world using light. "Photography" is a Greek word which means drawing with light, and early photographs were thus often called "light drawings." The most amazing fact about the "light drawing" was that anyone could create one, only if they had the right machine—a camera!

Developing a working camera, however, proved a difficult task. The first popular camera was invented by Louis Jacques Mande Daguerre, but it took him twelve years to invent a machine that could produce a photograph. When Louis Daguerre's new camera, called a daguerreotype, was released to the public in 1839, the announcement that it "requires no knowledge of drawing" made it an instant success.

However, early photographs were nothing like the digital images that take seconds to appear today. Daguerre's camera was a wooden box with a lens on one end and a slot for the metal photograph plate on the other. The structure was not very complicated, but the photographic process was difficult and required care for the images to be captured properly. The process was time-consuming, and the first photographs were bulky. Expense was also an important concern. Therefore, only the wealthy could afford to preserve their special occasions or become **immortal** through a photographic portrait.

New camera inventions and improvements to the photographic process changed all this. Soon, everyone could afford portraits, and now photographs are a very important part of modern life. Advancements in camera technologies allow us to see what people and places look like on the other side of the world. We can document historic events, keep pictures of sweethearts in our pockets, look at the surface of the moon, or peek inside the human body. Today, family portraits and books filled with photographs are common in households around the world.

_____ 1. According to this passage, photography was originally the experiment with

_____ .

    (A) glass   (B) light   (C) mirrors   (D) paints

_____ 2. When did Louis Jacques Mande Daguerre begin the difficult task of

inventing a camera?

(A) In 1639.

(B) In 1839.

(C) In 1819.

(D) In 1827.

_____ 3. Why was the first working camera an instant success?

(A) It was named after Daguerre—the inventor himself.

(B) It required no professional expertise as drawing did.

(C) It was sold at a price affordable to anyone.

(D) Daguerre spent lots of money advertising it.

_____ 4. We may infer from this passage that _____ .

(A) later improvements in photography focused partly on shortening the
photographic process

(B) Sir John F. W. Herschel contributed a lot to the modern camera
technology

(C) people in the 19th century used their cameras indoors more often than
outdoors

(D) before the daguerreotype, people had no way to record and preserve their
special occasions

_____ 5. In this passage, "become **immortal**" means _____ .

(A) invaluable

(B) living for eternity

(C) likely to be remembered forever

(D) distinguished throughout the country

Reading is a basic tool in the living of a good life. 讀書是使生活舒適的要素。

UNIT 11

The Tilted Tower

Even today, it is hard to believe that the Leaning Tower of Pisa, a 56-meter-tall, eight-story building, can stand for over 800 years in a tilted position, leaning about ten degrees from the normal axis.

Pisa was a major center of power in medieval Italy. People in Pisa wanted to build the tallest bell tower in Europe to proclaim their might. Work began in 1173, under the supervision of architect Bonanno Pisano. Soon it was stopped as they discovered the first northern tilt. Fearing the wrath of his compatriots, Bonano went into exile.

Nearly a century later, the architects tried to rebuild the tower by pushing it slowly to the opposite direction. But it was left abandoned again as Pisa went into war. At long last in 1350, Tommaso Pisano, a relative of Bonano, completed the tower in its leaning position by adding two extra steps from the seventh cornice up on the south side. On completion, the tower was regarded as a wonder of the modern world.

It still is. In 800 years, it has never stopped leaning. It leans at a steady pace of five arc seconds (about 1.2 millimeters) per year. For centuries, people believed that the lean was due to some flaw in its design. Now scientists have discovered that the problems lie in the soil. Erected on the shifting sands of a former estuary, the soil lacked the strength to support such a huge structure.

In 1934, the Italian General Benito Mussolini ordered to set it right by adding almost 200 tons of cement into the base, causing grave danger. During the nineties, the huge bells were silenced, and the stairs were closed to the public. Yet in 1995, the Pisan Government almost uprooted the tower when they began freezing the ground with liquid nitrogen in preparation for installing an invisible cable system. The tower started leaning south at an alarming rate of four arc seconds (about one millimeter) per day.

Ultimately, in late 1998, the soil replacement method was adopted whereby the soft soil from beneath the north side is being extracted and replaced slowly.

_____ 1. What is the passage mainly about?

    (A) The reasons why the Leaning Tower of Pisa was built.

    (B) The building materials of the Leaning Tower of Pisa.

    (C) The history of the Leaning Tower of Pisa.

    (D) The architects of the Leaning Tower of Pisa.

_____ 2. The Leaning Tower of Pisa has been regarded as a wonder because _____ .

    (A) it has stood over 800 years in a tilted position

    (B) it was built on the soft ground

    (C) it was the tallest bell tower in Europe

    (D) it was a combined work of many architects

_____ 3. Actually, the tilt of the tower was caused by _____ .

    (A) the flaw of the design

    (B) the wars

    (C) the soft soil

    (D) General Benito Mussolini

_____ 4. From the passage, we learn that the best way to stop the tilt is to _____ .

    (A) add cement into the base of the tower

    (B) add extra steps to the northern part of the tower

    (C) freeze the ground with liquid nitrogen

    (D) replace the soft soil beneath the tower

_____ 5. The word **wrath** in the passage most likely means _____ .

    (A) excitement

    (B) anger

    (C) challenge

    (D) confusion

The illiterate of the 21st century will not be those who cannot read and write, but those who cannot learn, unlearn, and relearn.
二十一世紀的白丁不再是無法讀寫者；而是無法學習、無法忘掉舊學以及無法再學習者。

Death-defying Daring

Imagine that you are in a barrel towed into the middle of the Niagara River. You are now moving at 100 kilometers an hour and slamming against rocks in the rapids. Then you come to the edge of the waterfall and drop straight down 52 meters. By the time you hit the water at the bottom of the falls you are traveling at 350 kms. per hour. You hit the water with bone crushing force. The shock to the body is incredible. You are probably unconscious now, if not dead. You are now one of Niagara Falls' famous daredevils.

The Niagara River flows between Lake Erie and Lake Ontario, forming a part of the border between New York State, U.S.A. and the Canadian Province of Ontario. On the river are a series of spectacular waterfalls. The Niagara Falls are one of the biggest waterfalls in the world. Imagine three thousand tons of water pouring over the falls every second. That is enough weight to crush any living thing.

The earliest daredevils were tightrope walkers, and the most famous of these was the Great Blondin. In the mid 19th century, he stretched a rope across the falls and walked across it while blindfolded. He also rode a bicycle across the tightrope.

It was not until 1901 that a person went over the falls in a barrel. Over the years 16 people have gone over the falls in a barrel and six of them died in the attempt. The last person to try was Canadian Dave Murphy in 1993. After that, both the Canadian and American governments banned people from going over the falls due to great danger. Besides, the stunts could cause damage to the falls because the rocks are very soft and easily broken. The stunts are now illegal and can result in a fine of US$ 10,000.

_____ 1. The writer develops the first paragraph mainly by _____.

(A) arousing the reader's imagination of an exciting trip

(B) describing the impressive scenery of the Niagara Falls

(C) giving examples of different ways to go over a waterfall

(D) using a quote of an extreme sports enthusiast

_____ 2. Over the 20th century, how many people survived the stunt ride over the Niagara Falls ?

(A) Sixteen.

(B) Six.

(C) Ten.

(D) Nobody knows.

_____ 3. This passage implies that going over the Niagara Falls in a barrel may cost either one's life or _____.

(A) one's money

(B) one's health

(C) one's reputation

(D) one's job

_____ 4. We may infer from the passage that _____.

(A) no one will ever attempt to go over the Niagara Falls in a barrel

(B) those who failed in their attempt to go over the falls were drowned

(C) tightrope walkers were braver than those going over the falls in a barrel

(D) the rocks as well as the force of the water posed threat to the person in the barrel

_____ 5. In this passage, a **daredevil** is a person who likes doing something _____.

(A) vicious

(B) dangerous

(C) spectacular

(D) illegal

There is an art of reading, as well as an art of thinking, and an art of writing.
思考是一門藝術，寫作是一門藝術；閱讀亦然。

UNIT 13

Keep It Real!

What would you do to win US$50,000? Would you, for example, bungee jump off a skyscraper? How about drinking a rat stew—the shake blends six rats into liquid? For all that money, would you then put your head into a glass case full of snakes? If you're tough enough, you're not alone; many have undergone worse things in the reality TV show. And millions more will watch you survive real, authentic, and nerve-racking challenges.

Reality TV is television that supposedly has no scripts. Reality TV programs feature not actors but ordinary people like you and me. They don't tell fictional stories like soap operas or police dramas. They show how ordinary people react when they are put in extraordinary situations. What the people on reality TV feel, decide, and say are genuine and have actual consequences.

Debuting in 1948, *Candid Camera* was believed to be the precursor of all reality shows. The groundbreaking reality show was MTV's *The Real World*. In this show, now in its 15th year, seven people are put into a house, and their movements are caught on camera for about 2,000 hours. The audience can therefore witness how people become nasty or kind to others. The *Survivor* series may be the most watched programs. In the show, 18 contestants are placed in an exotic location such as Outback in Australia and have to outlast each other as they endure primitive conditions and undergo numerous challenges. One contestant is voted off the show every week until there is a "sole survivor," who will get a million dollars for being the victor.

Reality TV sometimes affects people's lives in many ways. In *Wife Swap* and *Trading Spouses*, for example, two spouses from different lifestyles exchange places. Each will have to cope with a strange family, and eventually the both sides learn something about themselves and others. The participants reveal genuine human nature on the scene and make the audience think about what they would do if they were in their shoes. For the producers, participants and viewers of reality TV, the truth is definitely the only thing that counts.

_____ 1. Reality TV programs attract people mainly because they show _____.
    (A) famous actors and extraordinary scripts
    (B) the reaction of ordinary people in extraordinary conditions
    (C) interesting features of both soap operas and police dramas
    (D) all kinds of exotic resorts and gourmet food

_____ 2. According to the passage, the reality show has been around _____.
    (A) since ancient times
    (B) since TV was invented
    (C) for more than 50 years
    (D) only for 15 years

_____ 3. Among all the reality TV, viewers like _____ most.
    (A) _Candid Camera_
    (B) _Wife Swap_ and _Trading Spouses_
    (C) The _Survivor_ series
    (D) _The Real World_

_____ 4. We can infer from the passage that _____.
    (A) people will do anything if offered a handsome sum of money
    (B) being selfish is the key to win the prize
    (C) the show reveals most the bright side of human nature
    (D) _Wife Swap_ and _Trading Spouses_ may provoke most controversy of all

_____ 5. In the passage, the word **outlast** means _____.
    (A) argue with
    (B) fight for
    (C) support
    (D) beat

Every man who knows how to read has it in his power to magnify himself, to multiply the ways in which he exists, to make his life full, significant and interesting.
懂得閱讀之道的人能讓自己更偉大，也能讓自己的存在更有意義，讓生活更充實、更有價值、並且有趣。

UNIT 14

The Leverage

In the 19th century, Spain was a great colonial power. Its empire stretched across the globe, with colonies in Africa, Asia, and most of South and Central America. But, by 1898, due to successful independence revolutions in the Americas, the Spanish Empire was reduced to the islands of Cuba and Puerto Rico in the Caribbean Sea, and Guam and the Philippines in the Pacific Ocean. In the same year, the Spanish Empire collapsed completely due to the influence of one man, the American newspaper tycoon William Randolph Hearst.

Hearst, born into a wealthy family, began acquiring newspapers when he was only 23 years old. Seven years later, he owned a string of magazines and newspapers in all the major American cities. This gave him tremendous influence over the distribution of information. He was successful, in part, because he hired famous writers and was the first person to use color in his publications. Through his newspapers, Hearst became so influential that he brought down an empire.

Hearst got into a dispute with the Spanish government over land ownership and developed a fierce hatred for the Spanish. He used his newspapers to denounce the Spanish as backward, corrupt, and oppressive. He also encouraged support for the Cuban and Philippine independence movements. Hearst was so influential that when revolts against Spain broke out in Cuba and the Philippines, he was simultaneously able to persuade the American people to declare war against Spain in 1898. The ensuing war was won by the United States and the Spanish Empire finally ended. Guam and Puerto Rico were ceded to the United States, and Cuba and the Philippines became independent countries.

Hearst is the prime example of how powerful the press can be in shaping public opinion and molding events.

_____ 1. The subject of this passage is _____ .

   (A) the distribution of information

   (B) the decline of the Spanish Empire

   (C) the independence of the Spanish colonies

   (D) the influence of William Randolph Hearst

_____ 2. What is the breakthrough that Hearst made in publication?

   (A) He was the youngest newspaper owner.

   (B) He wrote problems between blacks and whites.

   (C) He introduced color publications.

   (D) He owned newspapers in all the American cities.

_____ 3. How did Hearst have something to do with the collapse of the Spanish
Empire?

   (A) He sold weapons to the revolutionists of Puerto Rico.

   (B) He induced the Americans to fight Spain and defeat it.

   (C) He led the revolts in Cuba and the Philippines.

   (D) He bought land from the Spanish government.

_____ 4. Which of the following sayings best sums up the main idea of this passage?

   (A) Pride goes before a fall.

   (B) We are all slaves of opinion.

   (C) The pen is mightier than the sword.

   (D) United we stand, divided we fall.

_____ 5. As used in this passage, the word **denounce** means _____ .

   (A) criticize severely in public

   (B) give approval openly

   (C) take land away illegally

   (D) make complaints officially

Learning is a treasure which accompanies its owner everywhere. 學習是寶，相伴一生。

Tourist Destination in Danger

From a distance, it appears like a shimmering jewel floating in a vast stretch of blue. The white marbled structure that pops out of every travel brochure and guidebook to India is sure to overwhelm you with its beauty and grandness.

Besides being an architectural marvel, the Taj Mahal has a fascinating romance attached to it and today's travelers do not want to miss out on that. It is an example of true love. A Mughal Emperor had it built in 1653 as an eternal resting ground for his beloved wife. Until now, it still instills a tender feeling of love into the hearts of the onlookers, and that is in a way causing its destruction.

Every year a multitude of tourists come to visit Taj Mahal, reaching an unbelievable number of a million a day on peak seasons. Overexposure is making the treasured site vulnerable, prone to damage. The visitors not only tramp the soft marbled structure, but they dirty the surroundings with so much litter as well. Some insensitive tourists even proclaim their love by scratching names on the stone. Furthermore, the fumes from the endless crowd of buses and three-wheeled auto-rickshaws as well as the cigarette smoke are eating away at the stones. Gradually, the marbles are losing their luster.

With the increase in the number of hotels, the tiny town of Agra has been stretching at the edges ever since. The over consumption of water and ill-equipped sewage system are drying up the ground. That's why the marble surface is showing tiny hair-like cracks at an alarming rate.

Travel broadens the mind and brings home the world. Yet, we must not forget that explosive growth of tourism may eventually destroy our treasured heritage and nature—things that cannot be reclaimed once lost.

_____ 1. This passage is mainly about _____ .
   (A) how Taj Mahal became a tourist's attraction
   (B) how tourism is destroying Taj Mahal
   (C) why we need to protect the ancient site, Taj Mahal
   (D) why the king built Taj Mahal for his wife

_____ 2. Taj Mahal was built over _____ years ago.
   (A) 1000
   (B) 1653
   (C) 350
   (D) 450

_____ 3. According to the passage, what are the causes that damage Taj Mahal?
   (A) Visitors.
   (B) Buses fumes.
   (C) Cigarette smoke
   (D) All of the above

_____ 4. Which of the following statements is NOT true?
   (A) The government has tried to repair all the damage on Taj Majal.
   (B) Some tourists scratched their names on the stones.
   (C) The marbles are losing their luster.
   (D) The visitors tramped the soft marbled structures.

_____ 5. In the passage, **insensitive** most likely means _____ .
   (A) intelligent
   (B) intellectual
   (C) thoughtful
   (D) thoughtless

Books and friends should be few but good.　書與友，貴精不貴多。

The Hottest Sports on Ice

What exactly is snowboarding? To some, it's a way of life. To others, it's one of the winter sports on the slopes, the one that has left many skiers wondering if they will soon be a part of history. Snowboarding involves the use of one board, to which both feet are strapped. The rider navigates the board downhill through a series of twists and turns, using body weight in much the same way as a skier does.

Many people think of snowboarding as a relatively modern sport, invented and made popular by teens who were looking for a way to ride their skateboards during the winter. However, the history of snowboarding dates back to 1929, when the first snowboard-like device was made.

That first "snowboard" was invented by a man named Jack Burchett, who attempted to secure a piece of plywood to his feet with clothesline, in order to ski downhill. This was the basic model for over 30 years, when the next major step in the sport took place. In 1965, the "Snurfer" was invented. It was a single sled-like ski with a rope attached to the front end for steering.

Since then, the snowboard has undergone many changes, including the attachment of bindings, which replace the rope and are used to secure a rider. Boards are also shaped differently, most resembling flat cigars, to make them more aerodynamic. Though it's been almost 80 years since the concept of the snowboard was introduced, it's only been in the last ten or fifteen years that the sport has really taken hold among winter sports devotees.

The sport really took hold in 1998, when snowboarding made its first major international appearance at the 1998 Winter Olympics. The sport has only become more popular since. Though many skiers today do not like the idea of sharing slopes with snowboarders, it has become common to see boarders at most major ski resorts throughout the world. It is accepted now more than ever, with over five million boarders hitting the slopes every year. Snowboarding is here to stay.

_____ 1. This passage is mainly about _____.
    (A) the changes of snowboards
    (B) the invention of snowboarding
    (C) the development of snowboarding
    (D) the comparison between snowboarding and skateboarding

_____ 2. The sentence in the first paragraph "they will soon be a part of history" implies that _____.
    (A) skiers will go down in history
    (B) skiing has affected sport history
    (C) skiers have made important records
    (D) skiing may be replaced by snowboarding

_____ 3. Which element is NOT involved in snowboarding?
    (A) A rider.
    (B) A rope.
    (C) A snow-covered slope.
    (D) A foot-strapped board.

_____ 4. What makes snowboarding more and more popular?
    (A) There are boards of different shapes to choose from.
    (B) Snowboarding has become an event of the Winter Olympics.
    (C) There are many winter resorts throughout the world.
    (D) More skiers have accepted snowboarding as an official sport.

_____ 5. In this passage, **aerodynamic** means _____.
    (A) able to move faster
    (B) able to afford
    (C) full of enthusiasm
    (D) easy to learn

There are two motives for reading a book; one, that you enjoy it; the other, that you can boast about it. 讀書動機有二：一是閱讀之樂，二是可以傲人。

UNIT 17

The Small Giant

Nanotechnology can create wonders in the fields of medicine. It works with atoms—the smallest units that all things are made of —in a computer-controlled environment. Imagine a fleet of molecular tools, much smaller than a human cell, enter your body to fight and safeguard you from damage and disruptions created by an army of germ producers. Justifiably referred to as nanobots, these nanomachines circulate freely in the body to determine the infected sites and eventually destroy them in such a sophisticated and precise manner that you will not have any clue about the goings inside your body. In addition, all you have to do is swallow an undersized capsule or allow a minor sting.

Like a robot, these nanobots can do anything. They can clean the cholesterol in the arteries before you fall victim to cardiovascular diseases. They can kill cancer cells or other life-threatening viruses that sometimes escape even the most thorough check-up. Painful surgery is no longer required—as these minute armies would heal and restore any dysfunctional organ. And you don't need to go for painful dental treatment; simple nanomachines would take care of that easily.

However, the most useful benefit of nanotechnology is its access to the exact location of infection, thereby lessening side effects, which may otherwise cause 100,000 deaths per year.

Scientists predict that much of the above is achievable in the next thirty years. While this has been laughed at, it may not be entirely a fantasy. Before long, an era of wonders and marvels would open up in front of our bemused eyes.

_____ 1. This passage is mainly about _____.

    (A) nanotechnology and its applications

    (B) nanotechnology and robots

    (C) how nanotechnology is used in the fields of medicine

    (D) how nanotechnology influences our daily life

_____ 2. How can nano machines enter our bodies?

    (A) By surgery.

    (B) By applying them to the skin.

    (C) We can swallow them.

    (D) The passage doesn't mention it.

_____ 3. From the passage, we know nanobots cannot function without _____.

    (A) a mechanic

    (B) a computer

    (C) a dentist

    (D) a blade

_____ 4. Which of the following is true?

    (A) Nanobots can spot and cure the infection better than sophisticated doctors.

    (B) Only after thorough check-up can nanobots cure the ill part of human body.

    (C) Without nanobots, surgeons cannot perform any surgery.

    (D) Improper use of nanobots may cause 100,000 deaths per year.

_____ 5. What does **bemused** mean in the passage?

    (A) Beloved.

    (B) Closed.

    (C) Entertained.

    (D) Puzzled.

Knowing is not enough; we must apply. Willing is not enough; we must do.
知不及用，思不及行。

UNIT 18

Less Boo, More Boost

In the United States, it is against the law for employers to discriminate against people based on their appearance or disabilities. These ideas came into law in 1990, through *the Americans With Disabilities Act* (the ADA). And they have since created extensive opportunities for men and women who once faced almost impossible odds in finding a job.

The ADA assists workers by causing businesses to hire people with disabilities based on their work performance, not their handicap, or lack thereof. The Act also ensures that people with disabilities are treated fairly and equally in the workplace by setting guidelines which businesses must follow in order to make a workplace more accessible to disabled people. Such guidelines might include the installation of wheelchair ramps, Braille numbers inside an elevator, and doors that open at the push of a button.

Many of the changes that were brought about by the ADA are so commonplace that today people without disabilities often do not give them a second thought. For instance, it is scarcely known that in stores, aisles have to be far enough apart to allow a wheelchair to safely navigate between them.

Though the Act has benefited millions of people in the United States, some business owners feel that they are forced to spend excessive amounts of money updating the office to accommodate people who may not even venture into their establishments, let alone apply for a job there. But if businesses don't comply, they stand to lose even more money in claims against them or face a hefty fine.

An estimated 20 percent of Americans suffer from some form of long lasting disability. That means this substantial piece of legislation is directly beneficial to around 50 million Americans.

_____ 1. The information in this passage is mostly about _____.
(A) how disabled people were discriminated in America before 1990
(B) how the ADA came into existence
(C) how the ADA help disabled people in the US
(D) how disabled Americans overcome difficulties in finding jobs

_____ 2. The *Americans With Disabilities Act* ensures that _____.
(A) every business hires disabled people unconditionally
(B) disabled employees are treated fairly and equally
(C) disabled employees get higher pay than the other employees
(D) disabled employees meet no obstacles in their workplace

_____ 3. Which disability-friendly installation or convenience is NOT mentioned in this passage?
(A) Smooth aisles in stores.
(B) Wheelchair ramps.
(C) Push-button opened doors.
(D) Braille numbers inside an elevator.

_____ 4. Which of the following is true?
(A) Disability-friendly installations are not common enough in the States.
(B) The ADA is so beneficial that disabled people no longer have problems in their lives.
(C) Some business owners do not obey the Act because they think disabled employees less efficient.
(D) Businesses that disobey the ADA are likely to pay a large sum of money for it.

_____ 5. "People without disabilities often do **not give them a second thought**" in the third paragraph means people _____ the changes ADA brought about.
(A) do not think twice about   (B) do not think of
(C) do not agree with   (D) do not adjust to

Learn as much by writing as by reading. 筆耕墨耘，泛覽群書都是一種學習。

UNIT 19

Toilet Tale

Access to clean toilet facilities is a basic human right, but according to the World Health Organization (WHO) and the United Nations Environment Program, more than two billion people around the world rely on shared toilets that are used by large numbers of people. With so many people using them, the toilets are hard to keep clean. Diseases spread quickly from these toilets, causing thousands of people to fall sick or die each year. These shocking statistics remind us of a mostly forgotten global disgrace.

The regions with the least access to toilet facilities are Africa and Asia. Throughout China, between fifty and seventy-five percent of people do not have flush toilets connected to a sewer or septic tank. In India, countless people have no toilet other than the bank of the Ganges River. More than one million liters of raw sewage enters the river every minute. The WHO estimates that ninety-two percent of people in Rwanda have no toilet facilities of any kind. With many people sharing small spaces, it is difficult to keep food and toilet waste areas separate.

Since the poorest parts of the world also need many other things, such as food, medicines, and education, the building of adequate toilet facilities is therefore often considered a low priority. However, many aid organizations, both in wealthy and poor countries, are working together to provide people in poor countries with access to clean toilets. In Mozambique, a local aid organization and an organization from Britain have joined together to improve hygiene in the town of Lichinga. They have begun replacing human waste pits with eco-toilets, toilets that use very little water and mix toilet waste with soil and ash to create fertilizer compost. Unlike the traditional pit toilets, these new eco-toilets do not smell bad, nor do they attract disease-carrying flies or mosquitoes. More importantly, they cost only 25 US dollars to install and nothing to maintain. These eco-toilets help prevent the spread of diseases and improve the sanitary conditions of people in even the poorest countries.

_____ 1. The passage mainly deals with _____ .

    (A) the poorest countries in the world

    (B) the invention of the eco-toilet

    (C) toilet conditions in poor countries

    (D) toilet conditions in African countries

_____ 2. Compared with Rwanda, China has _____ toilet facilities.

    (A) worse

    (B) better

    (C) fewer

    (D) dirtier

_____ 3. According to the passage, the poor conditions of toilet facilities brought about _____ .

    (A) lack of food

    (B) lack of medicines

    (C) the spread of crime

    (D) the spread of diseases

_____ 4. Which of the following is NOT the advantage of eco-toilets?

    (A) They are similar to the pit toilets.

    (B) They are inexpensive.

    (C) They consume little water.

    (D) They produce fertilizers.

_____ 5. In the passage, the word **hygiene** is closest in meaning to _____ .

    (A) dirtiness

    (B) sanitation

    (C) complexity

    (D) stink

Happy is he who has laid up in his youth, and held fast in all fortune, a genuine and passionate love of reading.

快樂的人，年輕時即已由衷熱忱的喜愛閱讀；無論日後際遇如何，這份熱愛都堅定不移。

UNIT 20

Terminal Tuberculosis Thrives

Two old diseases, tuberculosis (TB) and rickets have been returning to Britain. TB, a potentially fatal bacterial disease which severely damages the lungs, is a condition mostly remembered as a historic disease of the 19[th]century. TB was supposedly cured by the 1950s, but recent medical data from Britain shows that from 2000 to 2006 the number of reported TB cases rose to 1,790.

Like TB, rickets was apparently cured in the 1950s. However, the research by the UK Department of Health (DOH) suggests that rickets is occurring in one of every 100 children among immigrant groups. Rickets bends the skeleton and causes stunted growth in children for lack of vitamin D. This old disease can prove fatal like TB if untreated. Thus, it is very important to determine causes and treatments for both diseases.

Migration is the common factor in both diseases, although it affects each condition differently. The contagious TB spreads through the air when a TB-infected person coughs, sneezes or talks. Most migrants in the UK come from Asia, Africa, the Caribbean, and the Middle East, where TB is still active. Unfortunately, from the TB endemic countries to developed ones, the lethal disease travels with these migrants, who can then infect others they contact.

As for rickets, migrants from the sun-drenched countries require more sunlight to produce vitamin D and retain bone-building calcium. The cloudy British climate, however, does not provide enough sunlight for these migrants, who are also often unaware they can take vitamin D as a supplement to prevent rickets.

Awareness of any possible victims and effective action from the DOH are the best options for prevention and cure of both diseases. With antibiotics, vaccination, and efficient TB patient management, the disease can be eliminated from the UK. Meanwhile, the DOH can help migrants avoid rickets by informing them to get proper sunshine and to take vitamin D regularly.

_____ 1. TB and rickets that return to Britain have some features in common
EXCEPT that _____.
(A) both may result in death unless treated
(B) both seemingly disappeared from Britain for some time
(C) both are infectious diseases spread mainly through the air
(D) both have something to do with the movement of people

_____ 2. What is NOT mentioned about these two old diseases?
(A) Their causes.
(B) Their symptoms.
(C) Their cures.
(D) Their death rates.

_____ 3. According to this passage, _____.
(A) rickets had been extinct by 1950
(B) deficiency in vitamin D may lead to rickets
(C) rickets is a genetic disease specific to young children
(D) one percent of the children in Britain have developed rickets

_____ 4. Which of the following is a proper treatment for TB patients?
(A) Antibiotics.
(B) Intake of dietary calcium.
(C) Adequate vitamin D supplements.
(D) Sufficient exposure to sunshine.

_____ 5. What kind of country could **a TB endemic country** be?
(A) A country where TB is particularly and regularly found.
(B) A country where TB is the number one cause of death.
(C) A country where TB is extinct.
(D) A country where the number of TB patients is unknown.

They know enough who know how to learn.　懂得如何學習的人就是有識之士。

UNIT 21

Pros and Cons

Biosensors are microchips implanted into the body, and combine with wireless communications and global positioning technology to monitor body functions and geographic location. For example, Anne's mother has a tiny transmitter implanted in her body. The transmitter sends a continuous signal to a satellite, which analyzes the signal, and can tell Anne exactly where her mother is.

Biosensors can also monitor the glucose level in patients with diabetes. An implant can warn the diabetic when his blood sugar is getting too high or too low, so that the person can take remedial action before he becomes sick. A self-adhesive patch containing a minute probe is placed on the skin. The probe keeps the glucose level under the best control and sends an electronic signal to the patch, continuously giving the person his current glucose level.

Future medical applications in biosensors are endless. More and more information about a person's body will be able to be monitored, helping both patients and doctors treat diseases and extend their lives.

Non-medical applications of biosensors are also being on the way. Testing is now being done on a radio-frequency identification chip. With a microchip implanted into the body, sensors can immediately identify a person and allow them entry into a secure area, such as a military base or high-level government agency.

Although biosensors have to be thoroughly tested before being approved by the Food and Drug Administration (FDA), some people claim that the line between humans and robots is close to being crossed. They fear that biosensors can become too **intrusive** to a person, and that the devices may relay too much information, making it easy for unethical people or governments to control and monitor human behavior. Perhaps a set of guidelines should be drawn up to dispel their fears.

_____ 1. This passage mainly deals with _____.
   (A) how biosensors are made
   (B) why people need biosensors
   (C) the applications of biosensors
   (D) the disadvantages of biosensors

_____ 2. Biosensors are mostly used in the _____.
   (A) military base
   (B) government agency
   (C) educational field
   (D) medical field

_____ 3. The biosensor monitoring a diabetic's health is _____.
   (A) swallowed into the body
   (B) attached to the skin
   (C) not safe at all
   (D) not dependable

_____ 4. We can infer from the passage that _____.
   (A) biosensors have not been approved by the FDA yet
   (B) biosensors are not allowed to be used in the military
   (C) FDA is the first government administration to use the biosensor products
   (D) non-medical applications of biosensors have already been used in some schools

_____ 5. In the passage, **intrusive** is most close in meaning to _____.
   (A) intensive
   (B) aggressive
   (C) disturbing
   (D) expensive

The more that you read, the more things you will know. The more that you learn, the more places you'll go. 讀得越多，了解越多；學得越多，經歷越多。

UNIT 22

Venice: Sinister Serenissima

S himmering between sky and water, Venice is one of the world's most beautiful cities. Its nickname is *La Serenissima*, which means "the most serene." Yet, despite being a popular romantic destination, Venice has become increasingly popular as the setting for more sinister stories. British novelist David Hewson also sets crime thrillers in Venice. Hewson says it's because the city is very old and has "the very Catholic obsession with death. If you look at the paintings in those churches, they're not exactly full of joy."

And of course, the city architecture itself promotes mystery—haunted palazzos ("palaces" in Italian), crumbling villas, abandoned dockyards and labyrinthine, twisty alleys. Except for the occasional street lamp or TV antennae, Venice hasn't changed much over the past 400 years.

It was here that Shakespeare's Shylock, angry with the humiliations imposed on Jews, demanded his pound of flesh from *The Merchant of Venice*. Love and hatred, justice and injustice, ghetto and patrician—these have always been Venice's contradictions. Today, the upper class, the corrupt artisans and gondoliers and the newly arrived tourists and peddler immigrants are all characters provided for great stories. Venice is a handy place for a writer to pluck or release a character.

But modern Venice lacks space. Unless you are very rich or important, you can only be buried in the city's famous San Michele cemetery for ten years. "There was a disinterment happening the day I was there," recalls Hewson. "You could tell from the discreet canvas hiding the workmen slaving away in the sun...and the questions that popped into my head were these: what if someone who wasn't a relative turned up early and asked for a disentrancement with forged papers...? And what if, when the coffin was opened, there was something unexpected there?" His words really proves that Venice might look pretty and serene but it's a place where even the dead can't rest in peace.

_____ 1. The author depicts Venice mainly as _____ .
   (A) the most beautiful city in the world
   (B) the origin of Shakespearean plays
   (C) a popular setting for evil, mysterious stories
   (D) a place full of contradictions between old and new

_____ 2. Which is NOT the element Venice can offer Hewson as a thriller writer?
   (A) A romantic and serene atmosphere.
   (B) A strong link between death and religion.
   (C) Old architecture.
   (D) People from all walks of life.

_____ 3. According to the author, in Venice even the dead can't rest in peace because

   _____ .

   (A) Venice is overcrowded with tourists
   (B) Venice is sinking below the sea level inch by inch
   (C) there aren't enough graveyards for the dead
   (D) horror movies are shot near the cemetery too often

_____ 4. If a movie depicting the Venice of 400 years ago is shot, _____
   should be avoided.
   (A) winding alleys
   (B) Catholic churches
   (C) deserted dockyards
   (D) street lamps and TV antennae

_____ 5. In this passage **disinterment** means _____ a dead body.
   (A) burying
   (B) digging up
   (C) stealing
   (D) identifying

Never read a book through merely because you have begun it.
永勿讀完一本書只因為你已開始讀它。

The Eiffel Tower: A Daredevil's Dream

The Eiffel Tower has inspired thrill-seekers to risk life and limb, not to mention criminal charges, performing daring stunts at the famous landmark.

There's a long and colorful history of people doing wacky things at the Tower. In 1912, an Austrian tailor named Franz Reichel plunged nearly 58 meters from the first deck while testing out a parachute coat he had invented. Unfortunately, he never lived to improve on his flawed design.

In 1923, a bet-losing French journalist named Pierre Labric rode a bike down the 347 steps from the first floor. Many years later, his countryman, Hugues Richard, set the record for riding a bike up the 747 steps to the tower's second floor in 19 minutes, all without his feet touching the floor.

In 1984, British couple Mike McCarthy and Amanda Tucker parachuted nearly 280 meters from the top deck. Not to be outdone, three years later, New Zealander A. J. Hackett did a 116-meter bungee jump from the second floor and an American named Robert Moriarty flew a small, single-engine plane under the bottom arches. The same feat had been done in 1926 by a French pilot, Leon Coliot, crashing after being blinded by the sun while attempting.

On New Year's Eve of 1996, French daredevil climber Alain Robert, better known as "Spiderman," scaled the Tower's West face, reaching the top precisely at the stroke of midnight. He later downplayed the difficulty of his feat, saying "After all, the Eiffel Tower is just a big ladder."

Some risk-takers paid the ultimate price for their zany ideas. Others, like Labric, were arrested by police and charged after completing their stunts. Still others were luckier, and got off with a stern warning after promising never to do it again.

Perhaps it's the Tower's fame, something about its unique design, or just the fact that "it's there." Whatever the reason, the Eiffel Tower seems to draw daredevils, both brave and foolhardy, like a giant magnet which costs them an arm and a leg.

_____ 1. What is the main idea of the passage?

(A) The Eiffel Tower has long been regarded as the most appealing structure in the world.

(B) The Eiffel Tower has attracted daredevils all over the world to perform dangerous feats there.

(C) Some people enjoyed parachuting from the Eiffel Tower.

(D) Many people died for the Eiffel Tower.

_____ 2. What happened to Franz Reichel after he jumped down the tower?

(A) He earned a big prize.

(B) He was arrested by the police.

(C) He died for it.

(D) He paid a heavy fine.

_____ 3. According to the passage, which of the following feats has NOT been done at the Eiffel Tower ?

(A) Riding bicycles.

(B) Parachuting.

(C) Bungee jumping.

(D) Roller skating.

_____ 4. Which of the following is NOT true?

(A) Robert Moriarty flew a small plane under the bottom arches in 1926.

(B) Hugues Richard created a better record than Pierre Labric did.

(C) Franz Reichel was a stunt man so he successfully completed his task.

(D) The "Spiderman" did his stunt on the New Year's Eve of 1996.

_____ 5. What does the word **wacky** mean in the passage?

(A) Sensible.

(B) Worthy.

(C) Crazy.

(D) Meaningful.

Reading enriches the mind.　閱讀豐富心靈。

Give Them a Dog Chance

Dogs have long been renowned for their sharp sense of smell, which is said to be thousands of times as powerful as the human equivalent. In fact, when dogs are born, their eyes are closed and do not open for around two weeks. So dogs are forced to rely on their sense of smell in order to survive.

It is this extraordinary ability of dogs that has led to their use in important security work, such as looking for bombs as sniffer dogs. Dogs can detect the minute chemical traces of an explosive just by snuffling around a little.

Not long ago, scientists invented machines which could "smell" by capturing samples of the air and analyzing them. Bomb-detecting machines were soon introduced and some predicted that they would displace dogs in this role. The machines had many advantages. While dogs must be trained and cared for and have to rest every so often, the machines can be operated continuously by almost anyone. Bomb-sniffing machines are now in use in many airports, but they have not replaced dog teams.

Dogs are by far the best at examining large areas such as buildings or sports stadiums. The machines usually need to be presented with a suspicious object before they can operate effectively. Dogs can roam around, however, looking for things on their own.

The truth is that our technology can't yet match what dogs have naturally. In fact, we are still learning just how powerful a dog's sense of smell can be. Only in the last few years, scientists have demonstrated that dogs can detect the presence of cancer in human patients just by smelling their breath, skin or urine.

So, although technology continues to improve with each passing year, it seems that dogs needn't worry. We will still need those irreplaceable companions and their remarkable abilities for some time yet.

_____ 1. What's NOT one of the advantages of "smelling" machines over dogs?

(A) Machines cost more.

(B) Machines need no training.

(C) Machines don't need to be looked after.

(D) Machines can work longer without rest.

_____ 2. According to this passage, dogs are more effective than machines while _____ .

(A) working in the daytime

(B) working with their eye shut

(C) looking for bombs and other explosives

(D) examining a large area like a football field

_____ 3. In the 5th paragraph, how can cancer patients benefit from dogs?

(A) They can depend on dogs for organ transplant.

(B) They can depend on dogs for preliminary cancer detection.

(C) Dogs can comfort them and keep them company in the hospital.

(D) Dogs can sniff them to improve their chances of survival.

_____ 4. We may conclude that _____ .

(A) machines can never compete with dogs in any way

(B) machines will completely replace dogs' functions some day

(C) both dogs and human technology have potential to develop

(D) besides dogs and machines, scientists are searching for better ways to ensure security

_____ 5. The word **equivalent** in the passage refers to _____ .

(A) power

(B) nose

(C) sense of smell

(D) natural ability

We shouldn't teach great books; we should teach a love of reading.
我們不應該教導偉大的書籍；我們應該教導對閱讀的喜愛。

UNIT 25

As Blind As a Bat

Why are people afraid of bats? In many parts of the world, bats are considered the omen of bad luck because they are ugly, bizarre, and nocturnal; i.e., they are active at night. The dark figure of a silently flying bat can **incite** fear in many people even today. In addition, bats' queer nesting habit of hanging upside down creates distaste for them.

There are many misconceptions that people have against bats. Some people insist that bats collide with people and injure them, since they think bats cannot see well. Others believe that all bats are dirty and militant. Still others feel that bats can get entangled in women's hair and cause diseases.

There are also many scientific reasons for man's traditional hatred against bats. For example, bats have been reported to be responsible for spreading rabies. People believe that bats fly covering large areas and inflict the deadly rabies virus on more animals. However, scientists indicate that only a very small percentage of infected bats can transfer the disease to humans since rabid bats die fast. They also point out that the number of people who die of bee stings, dog attacks or lightning is greater than that of people who die of rabies from bats per annum. Stories of blood-sucking bats are not entirely fictitious either. A bat species called the vampire bat actually feeds on blood from warm-blooded animals. They attack sleeping cattle, dogs, horses, and birds with their sharp teeth, lapping up the blood from the wound. Stories of vampire bats sucking blood out of sleeping human beings are totally wrong, even though they are capable of attacking human beings. Perhaps it is this blood-sucking habit that has immortalized bats in numerous Dracula films.

In reality, bats are an important link in many natural life cycles. Various night-blooming plants especially need bats for pollination. Without them, these plants would simply die off. Bats are also excellent natural predators and can keep pests and insects in check. They are beneficial to humans in many ways and all the misconceptions that we have about them are actually unfair to them.

_____ 1. In this passage, the writer tries to _____ .

    (A) indicate the harm people have done to bats

    (B) correct people's misconceptions against bats

    (C) introduce some special types of bats

    (D) explain how harmful bats could be to humans

_____ 2. Vampire bats _____ .

    (A) exist only in fiction

    (B) help pollinate night plants

    (C) transfer diseases

    (D) suck animals' blood

_____ 3. Bats are beneficial to humans in that they _____ .

    (A) attack dogs with rabies

    (B) suck blood from sick animals

    (C) help plants to produce seeds

    (D) fertilize soil

_____ 4. Which of the following is true?

    (A) Bats tend to collide with people and hurt them.

    (B) Bats love to stay in women's hair.

    (C) People kill so many bats that they might become extinct.

    (D) People hate bats mainly because they cause disease.

_____ 5. The word **incite** in the passage means _____ .

    (A) rouse

    (B) describe

    (C) eliminate

    (D) dispel

The purpose of learning is growth, and our minds, unlike our bodies, can continue growing as along as we live. 閱讀的目的是一種心靈而非生理的成長，那是一輩子的成長。

UNIT 26

Smells Like True Love

ScientificMatch.com is a new internet-dating site created by Eric Holzle. Like conventional dating services, members must send photos and complete a profile with the usual questions about income, family background, religion, hobbies, and so on. Holzle's company goes a step beyond traditional matchmaking methods, though. Members of ScientificMatch.com also send a DNA sample.

Holzle's matchmaking concept builds on the "Sweaty T-Shirt Study" of Dr. Claus Wedekind, a Swiss researcher at the University of Bern. Dr. Wedekind assumed that just as animals sniff each other before they engage in a relationship, so do humans relate to the scents that their fellow humans exude. Then he carried out a study in which he asked women to smell T-shirts that different men had worn for three days. The women were asked to say which T-shirts smelled the best. With results in hand, Wedekind analyzed the DNA of both the women and men in the study. Furthermore, he was looking specifically at a set of genes, called the MHC or the major histocompatability complex. These genes make up part of the immune system, which helps the body to fight off illness and determines whether surgical transplants will succeed.

These genes, however, are the same ones that affect the smell of a person's sweat, giving everyone a unique body odor. Wedekind found that women with one type of MHC preferred T-shirts worn by the men with a very different MHC, and vice versa. In terms of evolution, that makes sense, since children of parents with a wide range of genes should have stronger immune responses, and be better protected against diseases. It doesn't sound romantic, but matching people according to their DNA might help find their soul mates.

_____ 1. This passage mainly deals with _____ .

    (A) a scientific study and its application

    (B) a breakthrough in evolutionary research

    (C) a special-designed T-shirt made of special fabrics

    (D) an unusual way to use smell to add to sex appeal

_____ 2. Why do members of ScientificMatch.com send a DNA sample?

    (A) It serves as a password.

    (B) It establishes their identity.

    (C) It carries all personal details.

    (D) It may help find suitable mates.

_____ 3. The "Sweaty T-Shirt Study" proves that _____ .

    (A) Dr. Wedekind's analysis only applies to single females

    (B) the smellier a person is, the more sexually attractive s/he is

    (C) the sweatier a T-shirt, the stronger the wearer's immune system

    (D) people are more attracted to those whose MHC is most different from their own

_____ 4. The passage suggests that children of parents with different MHC's _____ .

    (A) are healthier

    (B) are better-looking

    (C) have higher intelligence quotient

    (D) have unique body odors

_____ 5. The word **exude** in this passage means _____ .

    (A) pick up

    (B) give off

    (C) get rid of

    (D) count on

There are worse crimes than burning books. One of them is not reading them.
比焚書更惡的犯行之一：擁書不讀。

UNIT 27

Another Inconvenient Truth

There is much talk these days about global warming, but another problem causing concern is global dimming. Scientists warn that our earth is getting darker as well as warmer. Global dimming happens when air pollution reduces the amount of sunlight striking the Earth's surface. At first, this may sound like a good thing, as it seems to reduce the problem of rising global temperatures. However, the mixed blessing actually masks the truth of global warming.

Global dimming and global warming are both caused by the soot produced by burning fossil fuels such as oil and gas. In global dimming, the use of fossil fuels pollutes the air. This pollution then sticks to the clouds and causes them to bounce more radiation back into space; therefore, the sunshine to the earth is on the wane. Also, it prevents sunlight and heat from reaching the earth and makes the earth cooler than before.

Some people believe that global dimming has led scientists to take the real dangers of global warming too lightly. "It (global dimming) is an uncomfortable one," says English scientist Gerald Stanhill, who first spotted the astonishing doubled-edged sword and coined the term. According to studies, without global dimming, global warming may have caused temperatures to rise 6 degrees Celsius instead of just 0.6 degrees Celsius. Although it appears that global dimming offsets the problem of global warming, it actually does not. Worse still, it is preventing scientists from finding correct solutions to the problems we are facing now, or may have to face in the future.

As a result, scientists now suggest that people worldwide tackle these two problems at the same time by cutting their use of fossil fuels. The discovery of global dimming should serve as a turning point where people no longer bury their head in the sand, but bury themselves in solving the problems.

_____ 1. What does the writer try to convey in this passage?

(A) Global dimming does more harm to humans than global warming.

(B) Global dimming helps fix the problem of global warming.

(C) Both global warming and global dimming pose threat to the earth.

(D) Scientists should pay more attention to global dimming.

_____ 2. Global dimming may seem to minimize the problem of global warming in that global dimming _____.

(A) helps cool down the temperature of the earth

(B) absorbs more sunlight to the earth

(C) causes pollution to stick to the clouds

(D) traps more moisture in the sky

_____ 3. Which of the following is true?

(A) Global dimming, rather than global warming, is caused by air pollution.

(B) Global dimming causes the global temperature to drop 0.6 degrees Celsius.

(C) Gerald Stanhill enjoyed collecting swords and coins.

(D) Gerald Stanhill invented the term "global dimming."

_____ 4. The **doubled-edged sword** in the third paragraph refers to _____.

(A) the solutions to both global warming and global dimming

(B) the solutions to both air pollution and diminishing resources

(C) the problems of both global warming and global dimming

(D) the problems of air pollution and diminishing resources

_____ 5. What does **on the wane** mean in the passage?

(A) Increasing.

(B) Decreasing.

(C) Dazzling.

(D) Sweltering.

No entertainment is so cheap as reading, nor any pleasure so lasting.
沒有一種娛樂像閱讀一樣便宜，也沒有一種樂趣像它一樣持久。

UNIT 28

The Powerless Poseidon

Human beings produce a lot of carbon dioxide through the burning of fossil fuels. Fortunately, oceans absorb about one third of it, which blunts the effects of global warming. Nevertheless, the same balanced act may also force some marine animals to the edge of extinction.

Oceans are naturally alkaline, rather than acidic. This helps certain spineless creatures or invertebrates, including corals and clams, build their shells and skeletons out of calcium. When carbon dioxide mixes with seawater, however, the result is carbolic acid, which dissolves calcium.

In February, 2008, Andrew Knoll from Harvard University pointed out that the fossil record revealed the danger of acidic seawater. About 250 million years ago, the Earth experienced the biggest die-off of species in its history. The probable cause: massive volcanic eruptions that created a choking atmosphere of carbon dioxide. Ninety percent of sponges and corals became extinct. If global warming continues, by 2100, corals will face similar conditions and be unable to survive in the southern ocean.

Other marine invertebrates also will be in trouble. Gretchen Hofmann of the University of California has been studying the purple sea urchin, a small, spiny animal that lives among the rocks in tidal areas. Hofmann raised urchins under conditions predicted to exist a century from now if our carbon output doesn't change. The increased acidity of the sea water combined with its hotter temperature was deadly: The urchins had to work three times as hard as normal to create a skeleton and even then, their skeletons were often deformed.

The possible destruction of sea creatures such as corals and urchins goes well beyond their individual survival. The loss of corals, in particular, would eliminate habitat and food for many species. The effect could be catastrophic.

Given these grim possibilities, those who expect the oceans to ease the effects of global warming might want to think again.

_____ 1. What's the writer's main purpose of writing this passage?

(A) To voice deep concern for global warming.

(B) To show a fascinating natural phenomenon.

(C) To present the critical situations of spineless creatures.

(D) To point out the harm global warming does to marine life.

_____ 2. According to this passage, what is carbon dioxide responsible for?

(A) The alkaline environment of the ocean.

(B) The lower temperatures of seawater.

(C) Calcium being dissolved in seawater.

(D) Corals and clams being short of food.

_____ 3. Which of the following is true?

(A) Oceans are unrelated to global warming.

(B) Oceans reduce the effect of global warming.

(C) Oceans heighten the effect of global warming.

(D) Oceans will eliminate global warming sooner or later.

_____ 4. This passage suggests that _____ .

(A) eruptions 250 million years ago did not affect urchins

(B) urchins can be raised in artificial ways, while corals cannot

(C) urchins will be out of shape in hotter, alkaline conditions

(D) many other marine species depend on corals for food and shelter

_____ 5. The word **catastrophic** in the passage is closest in meaning to _____ .

(A) disastrous

(B) beneficial

(C) favorable

(D) irrelevant

Let us read with method, and propose to ourselves an end to which our studies may point. The use of reading is to aid us in thinking.
閱讀要有方法，並規畫研讀後的目的。閱讀的作用就是幫助思考。

Puppy Poop Preparation

It had been a long afternoon for Max. Shortly after lunch, his daily routine had been interrupted by two strangers. They took him on a long drive to a strange house. When he arrived, he spent a minute pacing in a circle around the living room. It was then he did something wrong. Max noticed the two strangers bounding towards him. One of them moved him aside, and the other knelt down and examined a brand new wet stain on the carpet. The two strangers did not seem to be very impressed.

I was one of those two strangers, and my first afternoon at home with my new puppy Max had not gone well. Within minutes of carrying this adorable eight-week-old puppy into the house, my wife and I realized that we needed to learn all about puppy toilet training, for the sake of both Max and our carpet!

We found out that new puppies need to establish an area known as their den. This is where they sleep. And all new puppies treat any place away from their den as a suitable place to go to the toilet.

Training began the next day. My wife and I watched Max carefully after his meals. Puppies normally need to go to the toilet between thirty and forty-five minutes after eating and, sure enough, Max began sniffing the living room floor just over half an hour after breakfast. I quickly picked Max up and carried him over to a corner of the garden, where he went to the toilet. I praised Max for doing the right thing and gave him a small dog biscuit as a reward.

However, I'd been lucky that first morning. Later in the day I didn't pay enough attention to Max's behavior. Max began walking in a circle, and before I reached him he had left a small poop on a rug. I was disappointed, but I didn't punish him for making mistakes because he might not have understood what he had done wrong and this slowed down the toilet training process.

By the end of the week, Max was making good progress. The docile dog gradually treated the whole house as an extension of his den, and only did his business in the garden.

_____ 1. This passage is mainly about _____.

    (A) how to set a new toilet in a house

    (B) where to set the toilet for a puppy in a house

    (C) a puppy's relationship with his new owner

    (D) a puppy's toilet training process

_____ 2. It took about _____ to teach Max not to poop in the house.

    (A) a month

    (B) a week

    (C) a few months

    (D) a few weeks

_____ 3. Puppies will go to the toilet outside the house only when they _____.

    (A) are given dog biscuits

    (B) are carried outside

    (C) treat the house as an extension of their den

    (D) know the house well enough

_____ 4. We can infer from the passage that Max is now _____.

    (A) a defensive puppy

    (B) an obedient grown dog

    (C) a stubborn puppy

    (D) a nasty grown dog

_____ 5. When Max **did his business** in the garden, he was _____ outside the house.

    (A) urinating and pooping

    (B) eating his meals

    (C) playing and having fun

    (D) taking care of his den

It is well to read everything of something, and something of everything. 開卷有益。

UNIT 30

The Sky's the Limit

The old kind of tourism is becoming rather stale and unexciting for many people. No more fancy hotels, strolling among ruins, taking photos of popular scenery, and buying souvenirs. Instead, they'd like to experience a different kind of exploration. They would certainly like to explore various cultures and environments, but they are more interested in self-discovery. Therefore, their vacations are called "adventure" and "extreme" holidays.

Adventure holidays are obviously action-packed. They usually involve demanding physical activities like hiking, trekking or cycling. The point of these tours isn't to make you feel relaxed or cultivated. They are to make you feel the rush of life by bringing you close to nature and actually experiencing other ways of life. For example, you can take a tour by pedaling through the Great Wall of China. If cycling is a cakewalk for you, you can opt for tough hiking. Some tour packages offer hikes up Mountain Kilimanjaro, "the roof of Africa." You can even take long bus rides across deserts or on the Silk Road. What would be your temporary roof over your head during these vacations? Usually it's a tent in the wilderness. Since adventure holidays are all about hiking, bicycling, riding local public transportation, and camping, tourists are not only tested physically, but are brought closer to the cultures thriving around them.

Extreme holidays, on the other hand, are more, well...extreme. In this kind of vacation, tourists are not seeking encounters with foreign lands and people. They are searching for places and situations that would challenge them physically, mentally, and spiritually. They seek out places where they can dive as deep as possible. They search for clear skies so they can skydive out of a plane. They are looking for high bridges from which to bungee jump. They snowboard down volcanoes at lightning speed. They raft in thrillingly raging torrent. They are into extreme sports so they can realize the limitations of their bodies and minds. In short, they perform all those death-defying stunts to feel extraordinarily alive, and to survive.

_____ 1. This passage most likely appears in _____ .

    (A) a recipe book

    (B) a recreation magazine

    (C) an instruction manual

    (D) a horticulture journal

_____ 2. What do adventure holidays and extreme holidays have in common?

    (A) Both bring holidaymakers close to nature.

    (B) Both make travelers feel relaxed and alive.

    (C) Both cost vacationers an arm and a leg.

    (D) Both offer opportunities to savor local delicacies.

_____ 3. The pronoun **them** in the last line of the second paragraph refers to

    _____ .

    (A) cultures

    (B) tourists

    (C) holidays

    (D) physical activities

_____ 4. Extreme holidays have to do with tourists' self-discovery in that

    _____ .

    (A) they travel domestically rather than abroad

    (B) their tours focus on spiritual exploration

    (C) they look for suitable locations to isolate themselves

    (D) they want to explore their own limitations

_____ 5. From this passage, it can be inferred that _____ .

    (A) the conventional tourism will disappear sooner or later

    (B) choices for extreme holidays are few

    (C) adventure holidays are unlikely to attract those who want to vacation leisurely

    (D) to take an extreme holiday requires more energy and courage than to take an adventure holiday

Read, read, read.　學海無涯，唯勤是岸。

A Sign of No More Sighs

Humans have an intrinsic need to communicate. Even the deaf throughout the world have developed a way to talk using signs and gestures. Sign language varies between countries just as any spoken language. Thanks to some devoted individuals, standardized sign languages for the hearing-impaired have been established.

In 1620, the first book on teaching sign language was published in Italy. Over 130 years later, Abbe Charles Michel de L'Epee of Paris founded the first free school for the deaf. In this school, he combined signs already established by the deaf with his own to form a signed version of French. His efforts paved the way for a standard form of sign language.

In the United State, Thomas Hopkins Gallaudet went to France to acquire sign language in an effort to help his neighbor's daughter in 1815. He returned with a deaf teacher and established the first deaf school in America in 1817. As a result of Gallaudet's influence, American Sign Language (ASL) grew to resemble French Sign Language (FSL). In 1864, Gallaudet's son Edward became the namesake and the first president of the first and only liberal arts college for the deaf: Gallaudet University. This college became one of the most important educational centers for the international deaf community.

In China, the first deaf school was established by an American missionary named C. R. Mills in 1887. However, Chinese Sign Language (CSL) was not influenced much by ASL. The reason for this is the difference between written languages. The English written language is phonetic—meaning that each character stands for a sound. Since many deaf cannot distinguish sounds, their signs grew from actions or ideas. On the other hand, the Chinese written language is pictorial, so the signs follow the already established pictures.

Despite the differences in languages, the deaf stay closely connected. A rich and complex culture has developed, with sign language at its heart.

_____ 1. What is the theme of this passage?

(A) Sign languages differ from country to country.

(B) Sign languages help people understand the deaf.

(C) The establishment of deaf community.

(D) The importance of the standardized language.

_____ 2. Chinese Sign Language is _____ .

(A) influenced by ASL

(B) influenced by FSL

(C) pictorial

(D) phonetic

_____ 3. The standard form of sign language was first set up by _____ .

(A) an Italian

(B) a French

(C) an American

(D) a Chinese

_____ 4. Which of the following is NOT true?

(A) Written languages have influences on sign languages.

(B) ASL and FSL have a lot in common.

(C) Edward Gallaudet was in charge of the first college for the deaf.

(D) Abbe Charles Michel established the first college for the deaf.

_____ 5. The word **intrinsic** probably means _____ in the passage.

(A) interesting

(B) innovative

(C) inborn

(D) intricate

Books give not wisdom where none was before. But where some is, there reading makes it more. 書本給的知識有限，但閱讀使其更充盈。

UNIT 32

Enter the "Ethical" Market

According to a recent research conducted by Harvard University, consumers are becoming more ethically-minded. A product with a label proclaiming its fair labor conditions has better chances of being sold, even it commands higher than ever price than its counterparts that carry no such labels. No wonder, companies take their Corporate Social Responsibility (CSR) more seriously now, than ever, to add to the appeal of their products.

Other statistics show that three-quarters of British consumers are interested in buying products that provide labor standards and possess "green" credentials. Products labeled attaining those standards are often selling like hot cakes. But are these consumers making the right choice? Unfortunately, all this ethical selling may not abide by conscientious practices. Many companies hide facts or even tell minor lies when it comes to making grandiose claims about the "ethical" or "green" badge of their products.

Going green is a growing trend worldwide among consumers as well as companies. Most consumers are happy to contribute to making the environment better. However, not many consumers will go an extra mile for this. They only want the "green" products that are of good quality and not costlier than the alternatives. On the other hand, if they can easily procure "non-green" products that are cheaper, attractively packaged and of decent quality, they will be happy to buy them instead.

The lesson here for companies that sell "green" products is to strike the right balance. Aggressively promoting "green" products as "environmentally-friendly" may not always sell. Consumers should be convinced both of their personal and environmental benefits. Consumers' personal benefits could include health benefits, energy savings, cost effectiveness, and so on. "Lower prices" still remains the major allure for most customers. Wal-mart seems to have hit the nail on its head when it proclaimed in one of its ads, "Earth-friendly products won't save the Earth if they don't save people money."

_____ 1. What is the main idea of this passage?

(A) To appeal to companies for more "green" products.

(B) To call on consumers to support "green" products.

(C) To cast doubts on the credibility of "ethical" selling.

(D) To present general facts about the "ethical" market.

_____ 2. According to the passage, companies pay more attention to their CSR mainly to _____ .

(A) raise their public image

(B) preserve natural resources

(C) gain competitive advantage over others

(D) help consumers make ethical purchasing decisions

_____ 3. The passage suggests that _____ is the utmost concern for most consumers.

(A) price

(B) quality

(C) social responsibility

(D) a healthy environment

_____ 4. We may conclude that _____ .

(A) products with "green" badges are inevitably more expensive

(B) companies that go "green" will surely make handsome profits

(C) both consumers and companies can contribute to a better environment

(D) it's impossible to strike a balance between consumer benefits and commercial success

_____ 5. "Wal-mart seems to have **hit the nail on its head**" means _____ .

(A) Wal-mart's words sound far-fetched

(B) Wal-mart has adopted a right policy

(C) Wal-mart's words contradict what it does

(D) Wal-mart overemphasizes its products in its ads

A book that remains shut is but a block. 書若不展，只是一堆木頭。

UNIT 33

Our X-files: Xaggerated and Xtraordinary

The unidentified flying objects (UFOs) have been a fierce debate for decades. There is no shortage of UFO sightings around the world. American George Filer writes about recent UFO sightings at home and abroad. One UFO was described as a flying black triangle with light in the middle beaming down. Another was a color-changing disk. Sometimes an object with mysterious lights can be explained as a small airplane or an overactive imagination.

On October 30, 1938, the radio play *War of the Worlds* caused an unexpectedly mass hysteria in New York and New Jersey. Despite the introduction in newspaper stated it was a play, thousands of residents asserted that New Jersey was being bombed and under attack by Martians. They phoned police stations seeking assistance in avoiding the gas raids and how to make good their escape from the city.

The show started out as an innocent dance program and then was interrupted with the special news flash that the Martians were invading the Earth, the same as real news broadcast would report. Some people were taken to hospitals and treated for shock and frenzy. One woman was reported to be **on the verge of** suicide, claiming she would rather die by her own hands than by a Martian's. The Police and other officials tried to persuade citizens that it was just a radio show and that there was no invasion.

One unexplained occurrence seen more than 100 years ago and continues to this day is the Ghost Lights of Marfa. Thousands of people in West Texas peer at the Chianti Mountains at night searching for the mysterious lights. There is no apparent source, no exact location but they move and glow. Some people say they are constant white lights; others say they are different color lights that move. Some see three lights while others see as many as ten. The lights have been investigated but they disappear when people get near.

Today, with such television shows as *The X-Files* and different specials claiming to be true accounts of aliens, the story of UFOs continues.

_____ 1. What does the passage try to convey?

(A) The occurrence of UFOs has proved true since 100 years ago.

(B) People are easily disturbed by the existence of UFOs.

(C) Martians' attacking the earth was just a rumor.

(D) Appearances of UFOs differ from place to place.

_____ 2. *War of the Worlds* was actually a(n) _____ .

(A) TV series

(B) scientific fiction

(C) play broadcasting on the radio

(D) actual occurrence in West Texas

_____ 3. Among all those different UFO sayings, one thing in common is

_____ .

(A) there is something harmful in the UFOs

(B) most UFOs are from Mars

(C) there are friendly aliens in the UFOs

(D) most UFOs show lights

_____ 4. Which of the following is NOT true?

(A) The Ghost Lights of Marfa have been investigated and proved true.

(B) The Ghost Lights of Marfa are still seen until now.

(C) The issue of UFOs remains controversial until now.

(D) With the special news flash, many people believed that the Martians were attacking the earth.

_____ 5. In the passage, the phrase **on the verge of** means _____ .

(A) mostly

(B) almost

(C) doing

(D) choosing

Develop a passion for learning. If you do, you will never cease to grow.
培養閱讀的熱忱；若為之，成長將不停歇。

UNIT 34

Selling and Smelling

Background music, visual displays and product samples work together to make a shop a pleasant paradise. Some businesspeople also believe that the use of the smells could help build up sales.

This concept is called "scent marketing," and it aims to attract consumers through their sense of smell. Shopkeepers use artificial aromas to create a mood, or even to reinforce the odor of the product the shop sells. These smells can be distributed by a simple spray system, but concealed shoebox-sized machines also exist to allow shops to vary scents.

Some research supports this marketing method. Martin Lindstrom, author of the book *Brand Sense*, explains that for 80% of men and 90% of women, smells bring back strong, emotional memories. This is because olfactory memories are stored in the brain's "limbic system," which is also the neurological home of emotions. Thus if smells are associated with a positive memory or emotion, they could encourage customers to buy a product, or at least linger in a shop.

Perhaps because of its association with childhood memories, a popular scent in shops is the sweet smell of chocolate. For example, an American cell phone store diffused a concentrated chocolate scent around a display of chocolate cell phones in order to create a pleasant shopping atmosphere in 2006.

However, not everyone follows to pick up the scent of success. Reactions to fragrances are highly individual, so what smells nice to one customer could provoke a negative feedback in another. Some shop managers also worry about polluting the atmosphere and even causing breathing problems for customers with medical conditions. But with signs, colors, and music everywhere, certain shops will certainly continue to try this method—if only to be different.

_____ 1. What's the main idea of this passage?

(A) Our brain has different reactions to different smells.

(B) There are innovative ways to increase sales.

(C) The use of smells could help increase sales.

(D) Different smells brought back different memories.

_____ 2. Which statement is true about the so-called "scent marketing" ?

(A) It is adopted by all the shops.

(B) It is founded on some scientific research.

(C) It is more effective than resorting to other senses.

(D) It is applied with the full knowledge of customers.

_____ 3. In the passage, how did the American cell phone store promote its products?

(A) By offering a discount.

(B) By presenting customers with chocolates.

(C) By spreading a pleasant smell of chocolate.

(D) By applying a coating of chocolate to its cell phone.

_____ 4. Which of the following is NOT true?

(A) The method only works on female customers.

(B) The smell might pollute the air inside the shop.

(C) Some customers could be sensitive to a particular smell.

(D) The smell might stir up some customers' negative emotions.

_____ 5. The word **aromas** can be replaced by _____ .

(A) brands

(B) samples

(C) colors

(D) fragrances

Reading furnishes the mind only with materials for knowledge; it is thinking that makes what we read ours. 閱讀提供獲取知識的材料，唯有思考方能獲得真知。

69

UNIT 35

The Mega Monolith

Rising nearly 350 meters above the arid desert and measuring 9.4 kilometers around, Ayers Rock in the Northern Territory of Australia is the world's largest single rock, or monolith. The spectacular rock formation contains various kinds of mineral, resulting in its magical color shift as the solar angles of incidence changes during the day. It was found in 1873 by a European explorer, who gave it Ayers the alternative name after Sir Henry Ayers, the Chief Secretary of South Australia. Over the next hundred years, the rock became a popular tourist attraction. Visitors happily tramped over its paths, making their way up to the summit. Few paid any attention to the "uncivilized," half-naked Aboriginal people who lived near the rock.

The early tourists knew nothing about the profound relationship between these original inhabitants of the land and the rock. Not until the 1960s when anthropologists studied these neglected people did the truth emerge. The Aborigines call the rock *Uluru*, and it has a central place in their mythology. The monolith is their most sacred site. It is the very center of the world's energy, where many ancestral, god-like beings lived in the "dreamtime," the time of earth's creation. Aborigines have preserved ancient cave paintings there, depicting myths from the dreamtime. The stones and boulders on the rock have special significance, such as being the actual body parts or weapons of supernatural creatures, frozen in time when the creation age ended.

Recognizing the importance of the site to the Aborigines, the Australian government made them the legal owners of the rock in 1985. The Aborigines themselves now manage it as a National Park, maintained by tourism and government grants. The Aborigines don't climb to the top of the rock, and they prefer tourists not to do so. Although many tourists ignore their wishes and opt to make the climb, more and more people are treating the site more reverently, coming there to wonder at this mysterious place, and share in the myths and culture of the traditional guardians of this magic rock.

_____ 1. What is the main idea of this passage?

    (A) The Ayers Rock finally became the biggest monolith of the world.

    (B) The Ayers Rock gradually became the center of the world's energy.

    (C) People gradually recognize the sacredness of the Ayers Rock.

    (D) The Aboriginals tried to ask tourists not to climb up to the Ayers Rock.

_____ 2. The Ayers Rock means so much to the Aborigines in that _____.

    (A) it was created by their god-like beings

    (B) it is the world's largest monolith

    (C) it attracts visitors and helps tourism there

    (D) it symbolizes and preserves the focus of the world's energy

_____ 3. The Aborigines organized the Ayers Rock as a _____.

    (A) theme park

    (B) national park

    (C) sanctuary

    (D) campsite

_____ 4. Which of the following is NOT true?

    (A) The Ayers Rock was found by Sir Henry Ayers.

    (B) Not until the 1960s was the significance of the Ayers Rock known.

    (C) The rock shows magical color changes during a day.

    (D) Many tourists there didn't show enough respect for the rock.

_____ 5. The word **reverently** means _____ in the passage.

    (A) respectfully

    (B) curiously

    (C) kindly

    (D) doubtfully

Reading is a means of thinking with another person's mind; it forces you to stretch your own. 閱讀可使人瞭解他人的思維，並拓展自己的視野。

UNIT 36

The Successful Sales Program

In-store television advertising has **mushroomed** in large retail outlets around the globe. By advertising directly in stores, retailers can remind customers of commercials they have already seen, introduce new products, promote sale items, and give more information about goods in the store. Furthermore, about three-quarters of buying decisions are made in the store, which makes advertising more and more appealing.

In this way, the world's biggest retailer, Wal-Mart, reaches customers with TV screens in over 3,000 stores across the United States. About 140 manufacturers lay money out to advertise on these screens, and data show that sales have risen two percent because of this promotion strategy. A two-percent sales increase may not seem like much until you consider that Wal-Mart brought in over NT$11 trillion in 2007. Tesco in the UK benefit in the same way—sales of some targeted specific brands increased by 25%!

Stores in countries with emerging markets are also adopting this lucrative method of advertising. The world's second-largest retailer, Carrefour, has already installed televisions in its stores in Poland and is beginning to do the same in Brazil. In Mainland China, an advertising agency called Focus Media is helping stores kit out this service.

Over the few years that in-store television advertising has been tried, companies have learned some things about it. For example, shoppers are unlikely to stand still for a traditional thirty-second commercial; spots of five to fifteen seconds work best. Also, ceaseless ads tend to frustrate potential buyers. To counter this, stores mix in miscellaneous bits about such topics as weather, entertainment and cooking.

In-store television advertising only started gaining popularity in the early 2000s. Despite a few statistics, no one is sure how well it works. As it stands, about 80% of companies advertising this way renew their contracts. So, in-store television advertising could be here to stay.

_____ 1. This passage mainly deals with _____.
   (A) the latest model of TV
   (B) consumer psychology
   (C) a new mode of advertising
   (D) Wal-Mart's marketing strategy

_____ 2. Which of the following is NOT one of the functions of in-store television?
   (A) It updates shoppers on the latest news.
   (B) It helps customers make their shopping decisions in the store.
   (C) It tells customers about the products and promotions in the store.
   (D) It gives manufacturers a direct channel for introducing their products.

_____ 3. Poland is mentioned in this passage as _____.
   (A) an agency in charge of in-store TV advertising
   (B) a market that is developing its purchasing power
   (C) a manufacturer with numerous potential customers
   (D) a country showing no interest in in-store TV advertising

_____ 4. In this passage, **mushroomed** means _____.
   (A) a type of edible plant with a round head
   (B) increasing and growing rapidly
   (C) going out of fashion
   (D) becoming more and more classified

_____ 5. This passage suggests that _____.
   (A) in-store TV advertising is innovative but impractical
   (B) there is no room for improvement as to in-store TV advertising
   (C) the strategy of in-store TV advertising leaves nothing to be desired
   (D) numerous companies applying in-store advertising benefit from it

The man who is fond of books is usually a man of lofty thought, and of elevated opinions. 愛書者通常也是有崇高思想或見地的人。

UNIT 37

A Shot for Clot

Hemophilia is a bleeding disorder. Normally, if we get hurt and start to bleed, the proteins in our blood cause it to clot. In people with hemophilia, these proteins are deficient, and they may bleed to death from a scratch or cut. For these people, however, the real problem lies in the bleeding inside the body, into muscles and joints. In serious cases, internal bleeding can happen spontaneously, without any apparent cause.

Hemophilia is genetic. The genes responsible for clotting blood are missing or dysfunctional. These genes are carried on the X chromosome. Men with hemophilia will pass this gene on to their daughters since females inherit the X chromosome from their fathers. But none of the daughters will have hemophilia since they have two X genes. To the males with hemophilia, their sons will not have hemophilia either, since they inherit the father's normal Y chromosome. In a female who carries the hemophilia gene, the chances of her passing the disease on to both her son and her daughter are 50%.

Hemophilia is also called the "royal disease" because it affected several members of European noble families in the 1800s. The eighth son of Queen Victoria fell victim to hemophilia and died at age 31, and two of her daughters carried the gene for the disease. One of these daughters passed on the gene to Tsarevich Alexis, the son of Russian Tsar Nicholas II, who was born in 1904. Rumor has it that it's hemophilia that eventually contributed to the family's downfall.

Thanks to modern medical science, doctors have created drugs that replace the missing clotting factor. When bleeding inside the body occurs, enough factors must be injected to create a blood clot. The development of replacement factors has made it possible for the victims of hemophilia to live healthy, longer lives.

_____ 1. The passage mainly talks about _____.

    (A) people who have hemophilia

    (B) the history of hemophilia

    (C) how to treat the patients with hemophilia

    (D) hemophilia and its causes and treatment

_____ 2. Basically, hemophilia is a(n) _____ disease.

    (A) tropical

    (B) contagious

    (C) hereditary

    (D) fatal

_____ 3. A woman who carries the hemophilia gene will _____.

    (A) develop hemophilia in her life

    (B) not develop hemophilia in her life

    (C) pass the disease on only to her daughter

    (D) pass the disease on only to her son

_____ 4. We can infer from the passage that _____.

    (A) modern medical science is sophisticated enough to treat hemophilia

    (B) only European noble families will get hemophilia

    (C) it's the father who carries the hemophilia genes to his son

    (D) it's hemophilia that contributed to the downfall of Queen Victoria's family

_____ 5. In the passage, **clot** is closest in meaning to the word _____.

    (A) proceed

    (B) thicken

    (C) flow

    (D) lose

The love of reading enables a man to exchange the wearisome hours of life, which come to every one, for hours of delight. 手不釋卷能讓人生活中無聊的時光轉變成美好時光。

UNIT 38

Grow a Gift for Gift Giving

There is always a birthday, holiday, or other special occasion to give someone a gift. As the world becomes more and more diverse, however, finding the perfect gift has become more complicated. Sometimes although your gift is well-intended, what it communicates to a person from another culture may not be well received.

Giving gifts in countries like Japan and Korea is culturally essential. Refusal before accepting gifts is considered very polite. And whether you are giving or receiving, using both hands shows respect. In Korea, giving sharp objects symbolizes a cutting of the relationship, and handkerchiefs represent sadness. In Japan, giving four or nine of anything is considered unlucky.

Countries in the Middle East have their own gift-giving practices. Most countries in this region have similar etiquettes because they relate to people's religious beliefs. In Islam, it's important to give and receive gifts with only the right hand. It is against Islamic beliefs to show wealth by wearing gold or silk, so it's better to take them off from your gift list. Moreover, pictures of dogs, which are considered unclean, could cast a cloud over the gift-giving activity. Luckily, it is only necessary to give gifts to the intimate people in your life. And a suitable gift would be a compass, which points the way to Mecca—the Islamic holy land.

People from Latin America are more laid-back. Only friends and family expect gifts. People in this region like to receive things they cannot easily get. For example, Argentina is a major cattle and leather producer, so receiving leather products would not excite them. Alcohol, on the other hand, is costly in Argentina; many people cannot afford it. Therefore, alcohol would serve as a nice gift. Things to stay away from are black or purple items. In Brazil especially, these are colors for mourning.

When it comes to gifts, it is the thought that counts. So the next time you give a gift, think twice to make sure your gift communicates the right message.

_____ 1. The author of this passage mainly intends to show that _____.

(A) the idea of a suitable gift varies from culture to culture

(B) it is very difficult to convey messages by means of gifts

(C) the influence of religious beliefs on gift-giving practices is universal

(D) giving gifts to intimate people is much easier than giving gifts to people from another culture

_____ 2. **Practice** in this passage means _____.

(A) an ancient legend

(B) a special price

(C) training to improve skills

(D) a widely accepted custom

_____ 3. Below is Amy's Christmas gift list, which item is suitable?

(A) A pair of scissors for the Korean exchange student in her class.

(B) A set of four tea cups for her Japanese tutor.

(C) A gold bracelet for her Islamic friend.

(D) A bottle of wine for her Argentinian net pal.

_____ 4. It can be inferred from the passage that _____.

(A) in Asian countries, receiving gifts without refusing first is considered greedy

(B) people in the Middle East prefer cats to dogs, for cats are believed to be cleaner

(C) in Islam, using left hand to give or accept gifts is considered offensive

(D) Muslim pilgrims can't buy compasses in Mecca

_____ 5. The author says that people from Latin America are more laid-back because _____.

(A) gift giving in Latin America is unworthy of a second thought

(B) gift giving in Latin America is relatively uncomplicated

(C) people from Latin America easily get excited about receiving gifts

(D) people from Latin America are so poor that they can't afford nice, expensive gifts

Read in order to live.　閱讀方能生存。

UNIT 39

Let's Dive In!

The word SCUBA is actually an acronym, meaning Self-Contained Underwater Breathing Apparatus. It refers to the type of equipment that divers must wear in order to reach the depths of the deep blue sea. Basic equipment that any scuba diver will need includes a suit to keep a diver warm, a vest, called a BCD, a tank of air, a weight belt to help the diver sink, fins, a mask, and a snorkel to use when swimming on the surface. Other items that divers may carry include knives, flashlights, cameras, gloves, and boots.

The underwater world provides divers with different experiences, especially a complete feeling of weightlessness when one is swimming beneath the waves. Besides, the sound of the bubbles that divers produce as they breathe is so captivating that one can never forget. Every body of water in the world contains a different underwater environment, and each provides something new to see. As a diver, one can swim with dolphins, search for treasure, photograph countless beautiful fish, and so much more.

There are many environments in which divers can go diving, as well. Tropical islands are the favorite haunt of divers, though shipwrecks and cold-water dives are also common. Each environment, from the water's surface to the sea floor, is home to different, fantastic sea life. In many places, though, the bottom of the ocean is impossible to reach by scuba divers, and machines have to be used to study creatures that live there.

Although the average depth of the world's oceans is 13,124 feet, the deepest scuba dive made to date only reached a depth of about 1,000 feet. A man named John Bennett completed the dive in November 2000, in the waters off Puerto Galera, Philippines. However, the average scuba dive is between 30 and 50 feet, making John's world record unbeatable.

With so much to discover under the waves, anyone who straps on a set of gears becomes an explorer. The moment a diver takes a breath beneath the waves, he certainly has something new to see and encounter.

_____ 1. What is the passage mainly about?

(A) The meaning of the acronym SCUBA.

(B) The general information on scuba diving.

(C) Some unbeatable scuba divers.

(D) Scuba divers' fascinating experiences.

_____ 2. So far, how deep has man ever dived?

(A) 50 feet

(B) 30 feet

(C) 1,000 feet

(D) 2,000 feet

_____ 3. Which of the following is true?

(A) "Scuba" refers to the person who invented the diving.

(B) Shipwrecks and cold-water dives are divers' favorites.

(C) With basic equipment, scuba divers can reach the bottoms of all oceans.

(D) People going scuba diving can experience weightlessness.

_____ 4. We can infer from the passage that _____.

(A) Scuba divers need much more equipment to go deeper diving

(B) Swimming with dolphins is most fascinating for divers

(C) scuba diving is dangerous

(D) scuba divers may suffer certain illness

_____ 5. In the passage, **captivating** means _____.

(A) astonishing

(B) being caught

(C) appealing

(D) dangerous

UNIT 40

Thought-provoking Tragedies

There are many reasons why tragedies have always been a favorite subject for playwrights, but the most important one is that they can influence the human mind more than any other emotional content. This is perhaps the reason why tragic heroes, both in literature and in theater, are one of the most remembered and endearing characters to audiences worldwide. For example, Shakespearean tragic heroes like Hamlet, Macbeth, King Lear and Othello are subjects of prominent theater groups the world over. These out-and-out tragic plays are performed more often than comedies and melodramas.

Another important factor that has helped to elevate the status of tragic plays among others is the fact that tragic plays, almost always, depict the lives of extraordinary men and women. While comedies are mainly concerned with the day-to-day lives of ordinary people, the protagonists of tragedies are often kings, queens, and noblemen who are supposed to be strong-willed and incorruptible. Perhaps it is the secret yearning of the masses to witness the moral fall of powerful people that makes tragedies popular. Conversely, tragic characters provide lessons for ordinary people to avoid causing tragic situations in their lives. For example, *King Lear* shows us the dangers of bad human judgment and *Hamlet* recounts how the prince exacts revenge with hesitation; *Othello* describes the dangers of envy and lack of trust while *Macbeth* speaks about the futility of hollow ambition.

Most people have the tendency to identify themselves with their favorite tragic heroes. They draw parallels between what they see in the plays and what they experience in real life. Thus, they often comfort themselves in the face of difficult circumstances, and gain a lot of moral strength to overcome adversities. Tragedies, in this way, have helped people determine the best course to be taken in life.

_____ 1. This passage deals primarily with _____ .

(A) Shakespearean tragic heroes

(B) the elements that make up tragedies

(C) the reasons why tragic plays are popular

(D) the contrasts between tragedies and comedies

_____ 2. What function do Shakespearean tragic characters mainly serve?

(A) To help theater groups gain popularity.

(B) To teach theater audiences some moral lessons.

(C) To prove how powerful and invulnerable noblemen are.

(D) To satisfy ordinary people's yearning for power and status.

_____ 3. Which description of the tragic heroes is NOT true?

(A) King Lear is a man of poor judgment.

(B) Prince Hamlet is weak and indecisive.

(C) Othello is envious and suspicious.

(D) Macbeth achieves a fruitful ambition.

_____ 4. According to this passage, how do tragedies benefit people?

(A) They make people shed tears and comfort them.

(B) Identifying with tragic heroes purifies people's souls.

(C) People find it easy to sympathize with others.

(D) People are inspired to face difficulties in real life.

_____ 5. In this context, the word **parallels** means _____ .

(A) similar features

(B) individual styles

(C) common interests

(D) typical characteristics

By elevating your reading, you will improve your writing or at least tickle your thinking. 提昇閱讀技巧，便能增進寫作或至少啟發思考。

UNIT 41

All Aboard the Orient Express

The British writer Rudyard Kipling once wrote, "East is East, and West is West, and never the twain shall meet." In those days, people in the West knew little about life in Asia, and vice versa. In fact, the only contact between the two sides usually came through trade, and sometimes war. The West once viewed the East as strange, exotic, and perhaps even a little abominable.

However, contrary to Kipling's viewpoint, oriental elements whet westerners' appetite for more stuff from the east in the 21st century. For example, Sushi and Thai food are now challenging pizza and hamburgers as the favorite dishes in Western countries. When it comes to decorating houses, some westerners are now getting into the craze for *feng shui*, the Chinese art of arranging furniture in a room or planning location and layout of a building to ensure happiness, peace, and prosperity. *Chi*, the invisible energy that is of central importance to Chinese medicine and certain forms of Chinese martial arts, is now becoming all the rage to scientists and doctors in the West. Some Western hospitals also jump on the bandwagon by offering Chinese herbal medicine along with traditional Western treatments.

The influence of the East on the West can already be seen all over the world beyond their own border. A growing number of Hollywood celebrities have taken an interest in Chinese herbal medicine. Also, many people are resorting to acupuncture to cure diseases or relieve pain. Those who are curious about martial arts are learning *t'ai chi*, an ancient chinese martial art that emphasizes slow, meditative movements. Yoga, a system of exercise from India, has become one of the mainstream sports today.

Ever since Marco Polo first introduced the East to the West, the Orient style and relevance have been a brisk business with Westerners. It is very obvious that in spite of progressing time, the eastern fashion still spreads the length and breadth of the world.

_____ 1. This passage is mainly about _____ .

(A) the differences between the East and the West

(B) the similarities between the East and the West

(C) how the West is capivated by the East now

(D) why the West wanted to learn something about the East

_____ 2. In the old days, people in the West _____ .

(A) showed negative attitude towards the East

(B) had enough information about the East

(C) were eager to learn about the East

(D) were very curious about everything in the East

_____ 3. According to the passage, the influence of the East on the West is most obvious in the field of _____ .

(A) literature

(B) medicine

(C) technology

(D) agriculture

_____ 4. Which of the following is NOT true?

(A) In the old days, the East and the West interacted only through trade and war.

(B) New technologies help promote the interaction between East and West.

(C) Yoga and tai' chi are sports from the East.

(D) Chinese herbal medicine has proved to be better than western medicine.

_____ 5. In the passage, the phrase **all the rage** in the second paragraph most likely means _____ .

(A) respectful

(B) memorable

(C) popular

(D) adventurous

By reading we enrich the mind; by conversation we polish it.
閱讀使心智豐富，交談使其更增光彩。

UNIT 42

Our Misunderstood Mate

Snakes are undoubtedly one of the most hated and feared creatures in the animal world. Many people find the scale-covered animal repulsive and make this concept deep-seated in their mind due to various reasons. According to the Christian faith, snakes are the messengers of Satan and are to be despised. Traditionally, snakes have been associated with evil in Greek mythology, certain stories of the Chinese mythologies and Egyptian folklore. Also, despite the advanced medical technology today, snakebites are considered a synonym of death in many parts of the world where antivenom treatment is rare.

However, scientists explain that less than 20% of all the known snake species are poisonous. Although venomous snakes have very potent poison, it is used as a means to immobilize and kill their prey, and humans are not the natural prey of snakes. Scientists believe that snakes take extra care to avoid humans and will never confront a human being unless cornered. Most snakebites happen accidentally during the mating and nesting seasons of snakes when they are most aggressive. One should know that most accidental bites occur when human beings trespass into their territory. Letting snakes be in their natural environment is the best way to co-exist with them peacefully.

Actually, snakes form a very important link in the natural food chain and act as a control mechanism that limits the population of rodents and small mammals. They control many pests and are considered to be the farmer's natural friend. In addition, a recent research has shown that snake venom may have a role in slowing down diseases like cancer. Lots of studies on snake venom are being carried out in many parts of the world to determine its possible uses.

Hence, we must understand that snakes are only as dangerous as other wild animals. If immediate and proper care is taken, almost all snakebites can be cured. It's amazing how the benefits of snakes far outweigh their disadvantages and threat to our life.

_____ 1. This passage analyzes the role of snakes in the animal world on the basis of
_____ .

(A) mythological stories

(B) biological theory

(C) scientific research

(D) traditional views

_____ 2. It is suggested that humans should _____ to avoid snakebites.

(A) receive antivenom treatment

(B) learn to identify poisonous snakes

(C) trap and extinguish poisonous snakes

(D) evade the areas snakes defend as their own

_____ 3. According to the passage, a snake is most likely to attack while
_____ .

(A) feeding

(B) making a nest

(C) shedding its skin

(D) hibernating

_____ 4. According to the passage, in which way can snakes benefit humans besides
being helpful to farmers?

(A) They may provide cures for certain diseases.

(B) They remind us of the dangers in a wilderness.

(C) They serve as moral lessons to purify the human soul.

(D) They make gourmet food for people all over the world.

_____ 5. The word **immobilize** here is close to _____ in meaning.

(A) chase

(B) scare

(C) exhaust

(D) paralyze

The best effect of any book is that it excites the reader to self activity.

書本給人最好的影響就是啟發讀者自我學習的動力。

UNIT 43

Distraction for Drivers

A study by researchers at the University of Utah has provided new evidence that the level of distraction experienced by drivers using cell phones is comparable to that experienced by drunk drivers. Perhaps surprisingly, the study also found that even drivers using hands-free cell phones were as distracted as those using handheld cell phones.

Professor David Strayer and his fellow researchers conducted their study with forty volunteers and four different simulated scenarios, which included driving without distractions, driving while using a handheld phone, driving while using a hands-free phone, and driving while intoxicated. The results of the study indicated that the likelihood of failing to stop at a crossing or being involved in a rear-end collision is greater for drivers using either type of cell phone than it is for drivers with no such distractions. Even the likelihood of a driver failing to see an object clearly in their view was higher among those using mobile devices. Professor Strayer describes the distraction caused by talking on a cell phone as "a form of inattention blindness, muting drivers' awareness of important information in the driving scene."

Roger Vincent of the Royal Society for the Prevention of Accidents elaborates on the behavior exhibited by cell phone users while driving: "You get sucked more and more into the conversation and you pay less and less attention to the road." He suggests a ban on the use of cell phones while driving and tougher penalties for violators could be beneficial. This study, in combination with the previous research, could help lead to bans on driving while using cell phones. "Previous studies have shown that you are four times more likely to crash if you are using a handheld or a hands-free phone," states Vincent.

The use of hands-free cell phones is currently legal in the UK; however, drivers can be prosecuted if it is proven that they do not have proper control over their vehicle.

_____ 1. What is the main idea of this passage?

(A) The development and history of cell phones.

(B) Using hands-free cell phones is legal in the UK.

(C) The use of cell phones, hands-free or handheld, while driving is harmless.

(D) The use of cell phones, hands-free or handheld, while driving should be banned.

_____ 2. We can infer that both Roger Vincent and Professor David Strayer

_____ .

(A) know a lot about cell phones

(B) oppose drivers' using cell phones

(C) take too much interest in the studies of cell phones

(D) experienced simulated scenarios in person

_____ 3. Roger Vincent points out that while driving _____ .

(A) the use of hands-free cell phones is less distracted than handheld ones

(B) the use of hands-free cell phones should be legal in the UK

(C) drivers using cell phones are 4 times more likely to have accidents

(D) drivers using hands-free phones cause less accidents

_____ 4. Why did the professor include "driving while intoxicated" in the experiment?

(A) To test how well drunk drivers can drive.

(B) To compare drunk drivers with the drivers who use cell phones.

(C) To prove how dangerous it is to use cell phones.

(D) To learn the real impact of using cell phones.

_____ 5. In the passage, **simulated scenarios** most likely means _____ .

(A) the assumed situations

(B) the real situations

(C) a play that makes people excited

(D) the summary of a play

People say that life is the thing, but I prefer reading. 人們總說生命無價，但我更喜歡閱讀。

UNIT 44

Beavers Bite

Have you ever heard the expression "busy as a beaver"? Possibly nature's most tireless workers, beavers are known for their amazing construction work. They **think nothing of** cutting down trees with their teeth to build dams which block streams to create ponds several meters deep. Not content to rest on these accomplishments, beavers then set about constructing their lodges safely in the middle of the new pond with mud, sticks, and rocks. Scientists have found that recorded sound of rushing water will trigger their instinctive dam-building behavior.

However, beavers' construction projects sometimes bring them into conflict with their human neighbors. When the dams break, the downstream land will be flooded. Besides, flooding causes damage upstream as beaver ponds expand, swamping what was once dry land. As a result, trees and crops are wiped out by flooding. Homes, highways and railroads all end up under water too. Human water supplies are contaminated by dirty floodwater, and sewers become blocked with sticks and leaves to the point where they stop working.

The usual solution is to destroy the offending dam. This is not as easy as it sounds. To the beavers' credit, their dams are built to last. One method is to make a hole in the dam using hand tools, and to let the water drain out slowly through the gap. For bigger dams, heavy digging machinery or dynamite can be used to do the job. These other methods often cover the downstream area with mud, silt, and debris when the dam is broken. The beavers' lodge is usually destroyed last, since destroying a lodge without destroying a dam is unlikely to make a beaver family leave.

As human settlements expand, people can't help but move into the beavers' habitat and wage a battle. Sadly, the animals seem to find themselves on the losing end. Sometimes living in harmony with these untiring dam-builders might mean putting up with some inconvenience, but beaver dams should only be destroyed when they pose a real threat to people's property.

_____ 1. The sentence "They **think nothing of** cutting down trees with their teeth to build dams..." means _____.
(A) building dams are normal and easy for beavers
(B) beavers are forced to do so
(C) beavers don't care how the finished dams look like
(D) dams are useless to beavers

_____ 2. According to the passage, what causes a beaver to begin its construction work?
(A) The instinct to mate.
(B) The sight of a stream.
(C) The smell of a giant tree.
(D) The sound of water in motion.

_____ 3. Concerning the damage beavers caused, which statement is NOT true?
(A) The downstream land is flooded.
(B) Upstream areas stay unharmed.
(C) Highways and railroads may be swamped.
(D) Problems with water supplies and sewers may arise.

_____ 4. This passage suggests that _____.
(A) destroying a beaver's dam with hand tools is ineffective
(B) tearing down a beaver's lodge without destroying its dam is not a permanent solution
(C) people downstream should be evacuated before a beaver's dam is destroyed
(D) a beaver's dam is not allowed to exist whatever the cost

_____ 5. What's the author's attitude towards the beaver?
(A) Partial.
(B) Indifferent.
(C) Sympathetic.
(D) Intolerant.

Reading makes a full man, conference a ready man, and writing an exact man.
閱讀使人知識淵博；交談使人處事機敏；寫作使人判斷精準。

UNIT 45

Sea Fans, Seeking Defense

Remember the dreamy image of a mermaid sitting on a pretty chunk of coral cooling herself with a sea fan? As a member of the coral family, sea fans are actually made up of colonies of tiny animals, or polyps, and are found in beautiful colors. Although they may resemble a fan to look at, sea fans actually provide a convenient home for sea life to live and feed in.

Sea fans are best known in temperate places like Australia and the Red Sea, where the conditions suit them well, but they are also found in chill sea areas like Norway and Alaska. In a protected place they can grow to almost two meters wide, but are easily broken by careless and reckless divers or stormy seas. In the best sites they can grow in huge groups that are called "sea fan forests." Despite being made of a hard material, the sea fan moves gently back and forth in a strong current.

Sea fans work like an underwater apartment building, with a number of other small plants and animals living in their branches. These small animals, which include tiny starfish, worms, sponges and sea urchins, catch their food as it floats past in the current. Imagine a small flat tree made of delicate lacy coral, attached to the surrounding coral by a strong thick root. This tree hangs out sideways into the current, often in a narrow channel running between two parts of a reef, allowing the animals that live in it to catch their food more easily.

Sea fans are very fragile and easily broken by storm waves that churn up the reef systems where the sea fans live. Although we cannot avoid some of the naturally occurring damage, we can definitely encourage divers and swimmers to be more vigilant when swimming near them. With care, we should always be able to enjoy these beautiful sea fans as we swim and dive around the coral reefs.

_____ 1. The passage is mainly about _____ .

    (A) the legend of sea fans

    (B) the living conditions of sea fans

    (C) coral reefs and sea fans

    (D) how to grow sea fans

_____ 2. Sea fans are _____ .

    (A) one kind of corals

    (B) beautiful sea shells

    (C) one kind of sea plants

    (D) food for sea animals

_____ 3. We can conclude from the passage that _____ .

    (A) only divers do harm to sea fans

    (B) the damage to sea fans could be prevented by some weather projects

    (C) we could do nothing but watch sea fans extinct

    (D) divers and stormy weather cause damage to sea fans

_____ 4. Which of the following is NOT true?

    (A) Colonies of polyps form sea fans.

    (B) Sea fans are not strong enough and breakable when storm waves hit.

    (C) Sea fans can't survive in cold sea areas.

    (D) Sea animals can catch food more easily living in sea fans.

_____ 5. In the passage, **vigilant** means _____ .

    (A) a ctive

    (B) watchful

    (C) critical

    (D) practical

Once we have learned to read, meaning of words can somehow register without consciousness. 一旦我們學會如何閱讀，一目十行就不是問題。

Get the Adrenaline Going

Wakeboarding, bungee jumping, and street luge are the three darling of extreme sports that push the envelope on sports. Also called action or adventure sports, extreme sports involve more risk, adrenaline, and personal achievement than traditional sports. They also come along with a whole new breed of athletes!

Action sports are actually the dangerous version of existing sports. For example, take springboard diving to extremes and then you have cliff diving. If you miss your landing during a cliff dive, you could break your back on a bed of rocks rather than just land with a clumsy splash! Extreme athletes experience fatal injuries while playing these crazy sports. World renowned professional, Mat Hoffman, takes cycling to extremes. He has had over 16 major operations and over 50 broken bones because of his sport. His most serious injuries occurred after jumping from a height of 23 feet on his stunt bike!

Scientists believe that extreme athletes are naturally designed for these risks. Adrenaline causes extreme levels of excitement and drives these individuals to do stunts that most of us can barely stand to watch. The chemicals that are released in the brain after they perform dangerous tricks make them become addicted to their sports and serve as the incentive for them to try again and again. To these athletes, a racing heart and the feeling of butterflies dancing in their stomachs make it worth the risk.

Extreme sports attract athletes who are obsessed with personal achievement and triumph rather than esprit de corps. There are few rules or referees in these sports, and therefore athletes rely on creativity, skills and fearlessness to achieve their personal bests. Unlike in traditional sports, these athletes don't care much about medals or winning. Reaching mental and physical goals is more important. After an event, the excitement from the young fans drives these daredevils to attempt even more difficult tricks. Sometimes, that's when the real show begins!

_____ 1. Which statement about extreme sports is true?

(A) Extreme sports are distinct from action sports.

(B) Extreme sports require courage rather than skills.

(C) Unlike traditional sports, extreme sports have no rules.

(D) Extreme sports usually evolve from other existent sports.

_____ 2. What do springboard diving and cliff diving have in common?

(A) They are both adventure sports.

(B) A board is the essential gear for both sports.

(C) The diver is vulnerable to the same high level of sport injury.

(D) The athlete is supposed to fall into water if landing properly.

_____ 3. Mat Hoffman is mentioned mainly to demonstrate that _____ .

(A) he is a world-renowned stuntman

(B) extreme sport is very dangerous

(C) cycling is an extreme sport

(D) he can surive 16 major operations

_____ 4. According to this passage, extreme athletes _____ .

(A) are driven by their nature

(B) care neither about medals nor about fans

(C) need coaches to train them to be more skillful

(D) set goals to defeat other athletes and surpass records

_____ 5. An **incentive** is _____ .

(A) a strong enthusiasm

(B) satisfaction that continues

(C) motivation that encourages people

(D) an exciting adventure

I've never known any trouble that an hour's reading didn't assuage.
我還真不知道有什麼煩惱是一小時的閱讀不能紓解的。

Giant Squid Finally Sees the Light

No one has ever seen a giant squid alive. Hiding in the bottomless and dark sea, they have eyes the size of footballs and have been reported to attack whales in the open sea. Though they are difficult to find, we know they lurk there from the stories told by old-time sailors, and by the gigantic dead bodies washed up on beaches around the world.

Doctor Steve O'Shea is a zoologist who has been studying these mysterious creatures for many years. He has taken long adventures to catch baby squids, which he then keeps in a carefully controlled aquarium environment to observe their habits and see how they grow.

Giant squids swim like jet motors, by sucking water in one end of their bodies and pushing it very fast out the other end. This, combined with their long thin bodies, makes them move like a torpedo through the water with their formidable and slippery tentacles trailing behind. At one end of their bodies, they have a strong beak-like mouth and five pairs of tentacles. The thinnest and longest pair is used to catch its prey, which is usually fish or other smaller squids. A giant squid would have to catch a lot of food each day by using its tentacles to fill its huge body.

Adult giant squids are believed to live about 500 meters below the surface of the sea. This is far too deep for most people to dive to. To study the giant squid's habitat, scientists have to use small submarines.

Not long ago, a massive squid carcass was found washed ashore on a beach in southern New Zealand. This 5.7-meter long monster weighed over 300 kilograms, and was in a dolphin's stomach. The sensational discovery was later transported to Doctor O'Shea's laboratory at the Auckland Museum. Now the authority on marine biology will be able to solve some of the puzzles he has about these giant creatures of the sea.

_____ 1. This passage is mainly about _____.
    (A) how scientists study the giant squid
    (B) deep water creatures
    (C) Dr. O'Shea's research on giant squids
    (D) the life of a giant squid

_____ 2. To study the habitat of giant squids, scientists _____.
    (A) go to the museums
    (B) observe on the surface of the sea
    (C) take ships
    (D) take submarines

_____ 3. Giant squids use their _____ to catch prey.
    (A) tentacles
    (B) beak-like mouths
    (C) tails
    (D) bodies

_____ 4. Which of the following is NOT true?
    (A) Dolphins sometimes eat giant squids.
    (B) The 5.7-meter long giant squid is now living in O'Shea's laboratory.
    (C) Nobody has ever seen a living giant squids so far.
    (D) Giant squids move like torpedoes.

_____ 5. In the passage, **lurk** means _____.
    (A) work
    (B) hide
    (C) stand
    (D) defend

To read without reflecting is like eating without digesting. 學而不思，猶如食而不化。

The High-flying Job

A pilot's life is ruled by strict requirements from the day he begins in-flight training. Only a small minority of students acquire full certification because the training takes an enormous amount of commitment and money. Not only are class seats very limited, but most flight schools also require a college degree and a clean driving record. Besides ground school and simulator training, many students have to become flight instructors so that they can afford to pay for the 1,500 hours of flight time that the average airline requires. When finally hired by an airline, pilots must get retested every two years. If they don't pass—to have excellent hearing and twenty-twenty vision—they'll have their licenses taken away.

A pilot has more responsibilities than an average nine-to-five worker in that he is responsible for the lives of his passengers and crew. Everyone on board puts trust in the pilot to take off and touch down safely and promptly. Bad weather, system failures, and security breaches are just a few of the major concerns that a pilot has to come up against. Besides critical non-flying duties such as balancing luggage and keeping logbooks, a pilot is in charge of a 50- or 60-million-dollar airplane that does not belong to him!

The schedule of a pilot is harder than that of almost any other profession. The average pilot generally works in shifts, not to mention working many days in a row followed by several days off, many of which are spent away from home in undesirable locations. On the other hand, senior pilots have more options as to which flight paths they want to fly and often schedule their own days off in warm vacation destinations. Unfortunately, it takes years of flying before these perks are enjoyed, and they are usually short-lived since in most countries, pilots are required to retire before 60.

_____ 1. The purpose of this passage is mainly to _____ .

(A) describe the rigorous requirements a pilot has to fulfill

(B) demonstrate the heavy responsibilities a pilot shoulders

(C) provide readers with a better understanding of the pilot profession

(D) impress readers with the demanding but flexible schedule of a pilot

_____ 2. According to this passage, which is NOT a requirement the average airline sets for pilots?

(A) Good eyesight.

(B) Excellent hearing.

(C) A clean driving record.

(D) 1,500 hours of flight time.

_____ 3. As far as responsibilities are concerned, a pilot is under NO obligation to _____ .

(A) carefully handle a hijacking by terrorists

(B) keep a close watch on the plane's altimeter

(C) check the weather conditions in his flight path

(D) check passengers' passports thoroughly

_____ 4. It can be inferred from the passage that _____ .

(A) pilots have to withstand both physical and mental stress

(B) pilots have a shorter life expectancy than average office workers

(C) pilots live the high life by earning an extra income as flight instructors

(D) senior pilots can transfer to another airline after they retire from one

_____ 5. The word **perks** in the last paragraph can be best replaced by _____ .

(A) locations

(B) benefits

(C) paths

(D) destinations

Learning never exhausts the mind.　讀書活腦。

UNIT 49

The Bold Charlie Brown

"**G**ood Grief!" That was the catchphrase muttered by the character Charlie Brown when things didn't work out as planned.

Created by the cartoonist Charles Schulz, Charlie Brown was one of the original characters in Schulz's *Peanuts* comic strip. Although Charlie Brown was assertive and mischievous when the strip debuted in 1950, he was soon developed into the lovable loser we know today. Using his own life as inspiration, Schulz molded Charlie Brown into a shy boy who had a unique way of looking at the world and a tendency to worry, prompting others to mock and take advantage of him.

Throughout the comic strip's fifty years' run, the yellow-shirted boy frequently failed. Each fall he tried to kick the first football of the season. But each time, his neighbor Lucy, who seemed to enjoy Charlie Brown's struggles, pulled the ball away just as his foot was about to touch it. Every time he tried to lead his Little League baseball team to victory, he failed, ending up with only two wins and nine hundred thirty losses.

It is easy to think of Charlie Brown as a pathetic character. His friends called him a "blockhead" and told him he was "wishy-washy." Even his dog Snoopy dismissed him as "that round-headed kid." Charlie Brown himself thought his life left a bit to be desired. He is quoted as saying "Sometimes I lie awake at night and I ask, 'Where have I gone wrong?' Then a voice says to me, 'This is going to take more than one night.'"

It may seem as if the hairless tot never did anything right. But this is simply not true. Charlie Brown's determination to triumph over adversity, his consideration for others, and even the way he handled his constant failures with grace made him a character that was loved and respected by his fans. After all, what better role model is there than one who refuses to give up even when nothing seems to be going right?

_____ 1. What is the main idea of this passage?

    (A) Why Charlie Brown is a loser.

    (B) How the character Charlie Brown was created.

    (C) Charlie Brown and the impact he has made on the readers.

    (D) The interaction between Charlie Brown and Snoopy in _Peanuts_.

_____ 2. Schulz created Charlie Brown based on _____ .

    (A) a legend

    (B) American history

    (C) his imagination

    (D) his own life

_____ 3. In the beginning, Charlie Brown was created to be _____ .

    (A) confident and naughty

    (B) pathetic and gloomy

    (C) bossy and stubborn

    (D) nice and considerate

_____ 4. Which of the following is NOT true?

    (A) It takes time and effort for Charlie Brown to make positive changes in life.

    (B) It is Charlie Brown's sense of humor that makes him popular with readers.

    (C) Lucy always tries to embarrass Charlie Brown.

    (D) Snoopy doesn't respect Charlie Brown much.

_____ 5. What does **wishy-washy** mean in the passage?

    (A) Determined.

    (B) Assertive.

    (C) Hopeful.

    (D) Indecisive.

Live as if you were to die tomorrow. Learn as if you were to live forever.
要活就要像明天你就會死去一般活著；要學習就要好像你會永遠活著一般學習。

UNIT 50

Sweat and Sweet

Have you ever imagined being a juggler, an acrobat, or a lion tamer? Obtaining those amusing jobs in circus is a dream for many entertainers worldwide. However, making it a reality means more work than play.

Like most jobs, auditioning for a part in the circus is a competitive procedure. While circus performers come from all walks of life, many have a strong background in gymnastics, dance, or theater. Hence, newcomers have a slim chance to outperform those circus materials to fill the vacancies.

Circus performers work harder than almost any other professional. Finding energy each day for training, rehearsing, and performing takes more than just wearing a fancy costume. Not only do circus performers have to be full of beans on a daily basis, but they also have to take good care of themselves. There is no room for error at the circus. Perfection is expected from the clown to the audacious tightrope walker.

Joining the circus also means accepting a life of travel. Along with being away from family for months at a time, living in foreign countries or a cramped trailer shared among many as home comes with the territory in this occupation. When the show is on the road, performers can work up to seven days a week, including holidays.

Unlike working in a law firm or doctor's office, the circus does not guarantee job security. There may come a time when the box office has to close. Then, circus performers must look for new circus employment, which means starting over from the beginning. Trying out for recruitment and making new friends is all part of the process.

As the circus gains popularity with the success of shows such as Cirque du Soleil, more and more people dream of working under the big top. It is an illusion that circus life is as glamorous as it appears on stage. However, if it's your true calling, you'll look beyond the heat of the lion's den for a chance to hear the crowd go wild night after night.

_____ 1. What is the main idea of the passage?

(A) There is more to circus life than meets the eye.

(B) The circus profession is a dream job for many people.

(C) It requires time and energy to adapt to working in the circus.

(D) It's hard to distinguish between the illusion and the reality of circus life.

_____ 2. Which of the following is true?

(A) A bean is the symbol of good luck in the circus.

(B) The circus provides equal chances for newcomers and veterans to join.

(C) Both law firms and the circus guarantee job security.

(D) Shows of Cirque du Soleil have been doing well at the box office.

_____ 3. According to this passage, which of the following is LEAST likely to make a good circus entertainer?

(A) A clown who is energetic and in good spirits every day.

(B) An acrobat who doesn't mind working a whole week without holidays.

(C) A juggler who is reluctant to move from country to country and sleep in a trailer.

(D) A tightrope walker who always keeps in shape and seeks perfection in his performances.

_____ 4. From the passage, we can conclude that the writer _____.

(A) is not in favor of joining a circus because it's more work than play

(B) tries to offer readers an objective analysis of the circus profession

(C) disapproves of the competitive and unstable circus profession

(D) prefers to watch a circus performance rather than audition for a part in a circus

_____ 5. The phrase **the big top** refers to _____.

(A) the thunderous applause from the crowd

(B) the large tent in which a circus performs

(C) the tremendous danger of losing one's life

(D) the highest or the most important position in the circus

The end of reading is not more books but more life.
掩卷時並不意味著將展讀更多的書，而是展現更多生命的意義。

ANSWER KEY

01. BDCBA
02. AADCB
03. BDABC
04. ABCCD
05. DBABC
06. DCBCA
07. CADBA
08. ADBDC
09. DCBCA
10. BDBAC
11. CACDB
12. ACADB
13. BCCAD
14. DCBCA
15. BCDAD
16. CDBBA
17. CCBAD
18. CBADB
19. CBDAB
20. CDBAA
21. CDBAC
22. CACDB
23. BCDAC
24. ADBCC
25. BDCDA

26. ADDAB
27. CADCB
28. DCBDA
29. DBCBA
30. BABDC
31. ACBDC
32. DCACB
33. BCDAB
34. CBCAD
35. CDBAA
36. CABBD
37. DCBAB
38. ADDCB
39. BCDAC
40. CBDDA
41. CABDC
42. CDBAD
43. DBCBA
44. ADBBC
45. BADCB
46. DDBAC
47. CDABB
48. CCDAB
49. CDABD
50. ADCBB

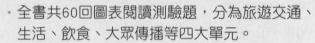

Advanced

★ 108課綱、全民英檢中／中高級適用

進階閱讀攻略

翻譯與解析

簡薰育、唐慧莊　編著

Main Idea

Details

Infer

Critical Thinking

Vocabulary

三民書局

READING POWER

翻譯

英語是承襲自撒克遜族和盎格魯族等德國侵略者所說的語言。盎格魯族所說的語言是「古英語 (Englisc)」，而「英語 (English)」這個字就是從該字衍生而來。隨著時間過去，其他侵略者如古挪威人和法國人所說的語言在英語中也創造出新字彙。因此，英語中有來自古諾爾斯語的「憤怒 (anger)」這個字，也有來自法語，同樣意味著憤怒的「ire」這個字。

除了字彙以外，英語也從這些語言中借來一些文法原則。例如，法語會在字尾加上「s」表示複數，因此大多數英語字的複數也是在字尾加上「s」來表示。然而，有少數英語字的複數形採用德語文法系統，所以「男人 (man)」的複數形是「men」，而「公牛 (ox)」的複數形是「oxen」。有時候一個英語字彙是由結合兩種語言的字所形成：將法語字「溫和的 (gentle)」和德語字「男人 (man)」加在一起，就產生了「紳士 (gentleman)」這個字！

在不同的國家使用時，英語也會發展出該地區特有的字彙、語句和風格。當英國在二十世紀中葉結束對印度的殖民統治時，這不只代表著歷史上新時代的來臨，也開啟了英語發展的新頁。藉由帶來如「loot」和「bazaar」等新字，印度語使英語變得更加豐富。除此之外，印度人一方面揮別英國統治，一方面卻歡迎他們的語言留下。「印度英語」這種混合了印度語和英語的混合式語言，如今在印度相當普遍。印度英語在印度廣告和電影中出現的頻率很高，甚至印度作家薩爾曼‧魯西迪也在小說中使用印度英語。今日，在各種印度語的自然音律影響下，印度英語有一種旋律般的語調。

有些語言學家認為，像印度英語及其他類似的語言現象是不正確的英語表現，但其他人士如哲學家伊凡‧伊利奇則相信，「一種語言若已沒有新變化可供學習，就表示該語言已經完全僵化了。」雖然英語在跟其他語言接觸的過程中產生許多轉變，它的起源仍是德系語言。

解析

1. 本篇只有第一段與第二段述及英文的起源，全篇的重點是強調英文是大雜燴，許多國家的語言對英文都有影響，尤其文末 **English has changed through contact with other languages...**，故選(B)其他國家的語言對英語的影響。

2. 由第一段 The **Angles** spoke "Englisc," and it is from this word that the word "English" itself is derived 可知答案是(D)盎格魯族。

3. Hinglish 即是 Hindu 與 English 的混合，故選(C)。ox 的複數 oxen 是根據日耳曼語系 (Germanic system) 而非法文，(A)為非；ire 來自於法文而非印度文，(B)為非；由文末 its origins are still Germanic 可知來源是日耳曼，(D)為非。

4. 由第二段可知英語的複數大部分根據法文來做變化，不過有少部分根據日耳曼語系，故(B)所有的名詞都是根據法文來做複數變化為非。

5. 關鍵字前一句中的 **mixture** 即是推測本單字最好的線索，故選(A)。

---

coin vt. 創造 (新字)　　ire n. 憤怒　　govern vt. 支配　　loot vi./vt. 搶奪　　bazaar n. 市集
callous adj. 冷酷無感覺的

我們的毛茸茸朋友
Our Furry Friends

翻譯

　　北極熊居住在北極，一個由冰和雪所構成的嚴峻世界，只有少數生物能在那裡存活。北極熊不會冬眠，一整年都是他們的活動時期，許多時間甚至是在冰冷的水中度過。他們是怎麼做到的？答案就在那一身厚厚的白色毛皮和底下的特殊皮膚裡。

　　白色毛皮讓北極熊能融入北方極地的雪白環境中，使這種陸地上最大的掠食動物能隱藏自己的身形，神不知鬼不覺地撲上獵物。此外，白色毛皮也能在北極熊發現自己成為獵物時成為牠們的保護色。但事實上，這身外套般的毛皮，是牠們抵禦惡劣氣候的第一道防線。

　　北極熊這身毛皮外套的最外層是由粗硬的毛幹構成，這些毛幹部分是空心而且透明的，看起來很像細細的吸管。它們會反射陽光，使毛皮看起來是白色。中間的空心部分能使空氣被滯留在裡面，形成隔絕低溫所必須的隔離層。這些毛幹的另一個重要特性在於它們不會纏結在一起，因此北極熊能輕易地把水、雪和冰從毛皮上甩掉。北極熊抵禦嚴寒環境的第二道防線是在外層毛幹之下那層厚如羊毛，能為牠們提供更多保暖作用的內層絨毛。

　　在這片白色毛皮底下，北極熊的皮膚實際上是黑色，有助於吸收並保留來自陽光的溫暖，而不是將其反射出去。北極熊跟鯨魚和海豹一樣，在皮膚底下有一層被稱為鯨脂的厚厚脂肪，是更佳的低溫隔絕層。

　　所有動物都必須適應自身所在的生存環境，而北極熊所面對的挑戰尤其嚴厲。在北極大地上，只有強者能生存。但有著一身白色毛皮、黑色皮膚和一層鯨脂的北極熊，把這片荒涼大地變成了自己的家。

解析

1. 文章最後一段第二句提到唯有強者方能在北極生存。而北極熊又因具有三層保暖的條件，所以能以北極為家，故答案選(A)適者生存。
2. 由第一段 Polar bears don't hibernate 得知北極熊不冬眠，牠們整年保持活動，故(A)它們整個冬天都在睡覺維持體力為錯為錯。
3. 根據文章第三段提到北極熊的毛不會糾結，所以很容易把水和冰雪抖落，所以答案選(D)。
4. 本題考文章細節。第四段提到北極熊的皮膚實際上是黑色的，所以答案是(C)。(A)(B)(D)均沒有提到。
5. 第二段提到當北極熊發現自己被追捕時，白色皮毛可在雪地裡提供保護色，可見這是(B)使北極熊難以被發現的方法。

the Arctic 北極圈　　forbidding adj. 令人害怕的　　hibernate vi. 冬眠　　predator n. 食肉動物，掠食者
hair shaft n. 毛幹　　transparent adj. 透明的　　insulation n. 隔離　　matted adj. 糾結的
blubber n. 鯨脂

一窺羅托魯阿
A Quick Glimpse of Rotorua

翻譯

踏入這座寧靜小鎮的那一刻起，你就知道自己身在某個很不一樣的地方。似煙的縷縷蒸汽自各處升起——公園、街道上或建築物後方——使深藍色的天空籠罩在一片灰色雲霧中。濃烈的硫磺臭味飄溢在原本可能滿是清新晨露香味的空氣中，間歇泉自地底下猛烈噴出沸騰熱水，一灘灘的泥漿則不斷冒著泡。羅托魯阿，一座位於紐西蘭北島的城鎮，以謙卑的肩頭承載著大自然憤怒的遺產。

這座小鎮是毛利文化的搖籃。在毛利語中，「羅托 (roto)」意指「湖」，而「魯阿 (rua)」則意指「二」，因為這裡是毛利族酋長伊罕加西和族人在十四世紀抵達此地時所發現的第二大湖。

在此地絕不能錯過的景觀是每天噴發的納克斯女士間歇泉。從每天早上十點三十分開始，熱水噴泉會從一個灰色小丘頂端噴出約一小時之久。它是這個地區的生命之閥，形同累積在這一帶地殼下壓力的排氣孔，否則這些壓力隨時可能造成致命的災難。觀光局巧妙地控制噴發時間，使這座間歇泉成為最熱門的觀光景點。他們運用簡單的科學原理，將鹽加入噴發口，使表面壓力下降，於是底下的水就會湧上噴出。

另一個主要觀光地區是懷芒古火山谷，它有段悲傷的過去。1886 年，塔拉威拉火山爆發，使這片地區整個被熾熱的熔岩、石頭和火山灰所覆蓋。轉眼之間，附近的村莊就被埋在毀滅一切的火山碎屑之下。許多年後，此處遺跡才被挖掘出土。各個地點——市場、學校及餐廳——看起來就像它們還處於日常的繁忙活動之中，只是居民們突然決定表演戲法把自己變不見了。

在羅托魯阿，你可以感受到大自然情緒的力量。她無法控制自己的憤怒，不時將悲慘與不幸帶來這片大地。但大自然因此所形成的美麗地景，卻也展現出她的愛與關懷。

解析

1. 本題旨在測驗主旨大意，(A)(C)(D)選項的敘述僅觸及各段重點，只有(B)的敘述涵蓋全篇大意。

2. 第一段敘述步入羅托魯阿即可看見溫泉的煙霧並聞到其硫磺味，可推論其最大的特色在於當地的溫泉，故選(D)。羅托魯阿雖是毛利文化的搖籃，此乃歷史，屬本文的細節之一，且本文對此特點著墨不多，故不選(A)；(B)為作者敘述的比喻；(C)指懷芒古火山谷。

3. 觀光客並未因塔拉威拉火山曾爆發而不去懷芒古火山谷觀光，故選(A)。

4. 本題考文章推理，塔拉威拉火山突然爆發，瞬間帶走一切生命，顯見大自然的威力，故選(B)。

5. the magician 指大自然瞬間變換掃蕩的威力，使一切瞬間消失殆盡，故選(C)。

---

sulfur n. 硫磺　　geyser n. 間歇泉　　mound n. 土堆；小丘　　coil vt. 盤繞　　debris n. 殘骸

翻譯

　　1980 年代中期，世界上所有人似乎突然變成了美國人。人們不是跟著從許多收音機喇叭中大聲播放出來的聲音一起唱，就是用腳跟著打節拍。那個聲音一遍又一遍地唱著：「我生於美國，我生於美國。」隨著這首歌、同名專輯，以及那滄桑但帶著傲氣的聲音，布魯斯‧史普林斯汀來到世人面前。

　　《生於美國》這張專輯中有七首暢銷單曲，全球總計賣出超過一千萬張，使這名紐澤西州出生的搖滾歌手及流行歌曲作者成為世人偶像。但即使持續受到歡迎，史普林斯汀卻遭到很大程度上的誤解。史普林斯汀很快就被視為美國自大的象徵。許多人對〈生於美國〉這首歌舉雙手贊成，有無數其他人認為歌曲中類似聖歌的節拍和歌詞太美國化，太趾高氣昂。但只要仔細聽過歌詞的人就會知道，事情並非如此。在這首歌中，史普林斯汀描述一名男子「勞碌奔波了十年／既無法逃離也沒有未來可言。」因此他並未歌頌美國，而是對美國提出社會批判。

　　自從 1970 年代開始，史普林斯汀就開始唱出平民百姓希望，夢想的達成及令人震驚的生活經驗。工廠工人、店員和弱勢者是史普林斯汀代為發聲的對象。他在〈生為逃離〉這首歌中給予小鎮青少年希望：「我們必須趁年輕時離開這裡／因為像我們這樣的流浪者，生來就是為了要逃離」；他也在〈湯姆喬德之魂〉這首歌中唱出美國藍領階級移民的困境；在〈費城街道〉這首歌中描寫愛滋病。至今幾十年來，史普林斯汀已為一些美國人唱出他們通常不為人知的故事。他對美國的描述——一片做夢和遭受挫折的土地——為他贏得全球許多歌迷支持，因為他們跟他的曲中人物一樣，經歷著同樣的希望和悲傷。如今已六十出頭的史普林斯汀創作力未曾稍減。他的暢銷專輯《躍昇》主要描述因 911 事件而改變及失去的百姓生活，史普林斯汀唱道：「願仍活著的人敞開心胸讓我們加入，使我們不被死亡的悲傷所擊垮。」讓我們一起期望這個世界會繼續傾聽下去。

解析

1. 本題考文章理解。第三段提到史普林斯汀為各行各業市井小民發聲，並列出某首歌的某句歌詞，舉例證明他其實並非一昧歌頌美國，故選(A)。

2. 本題考文章細節。根據第二段最後一句 He does not glorify America, but offers social criticism about it 得知答案為(B)提出關於美國社會問題的評論。

3. 根據第三段提到他在〈湯姆喬德之魂〉這首歌裡唱到美國藍領階級移民的困境，故選(C)。

4. 第三段提到歌迷可以和史普林斯汀歌中的人物分享同樣的希望和苦惱，也就是能夠認同 (identify with) 歌中的人物，故選(C)。

5. 第二段說到由於〈生於美國〉使得史普林斯汀被鑄造成美國傲慢自大 (arrogance) 的象徵。因此 cocky 可以和(D)妄自尊大代換。

tap　vt.　(附和著節拍) 輕拍，輕叩　　blare　vt.　發出響而刺耳的聲音　　shattering　adj.　令人震驚的
plight　n.　困境

O5 黏到天長地久
Stuck On Glues

翻譯

　　黏膠也許是人類使用最久的人造物品。事實上，黏膠一直隨著人類的發展同步演進。

　　巴比倫人也許是最早將黏膠作為黏著物質使用的人。他們用動物製的膠來修復破掉的器皿。記錄顯示四千年前古代埃及人製作傢俱時就用到黏膠。他們使用從獸皮和動物皮膚上取得的獸皮膠。獸皮膠一直被視為一項重大發現，直到羅馬人和希臘人開始用魚膠將薄木片黏在一起。木工製品需要黏力更強的黏膠，因此導致魚膠的發展。

　　即便黏膠科技在許多國家和早期文明已有相當演進，許多黏膠的成分至今仍不明。例如，成吉思汗和他的軍隊所開發和使用的黏膠以其黏著力聞名，但沒有人知道他的秘密配方到底是什麼。中世紀時，黏膠被運用在製作傢俱和樂器上，也被用在建築、釣魚和戰爭中。

　　1750 年左右，荷蘭開始工業化生產黏膠，它也是第一個擁有商業化黏膠工廠的國家。英國是第一個對某種魚膠發出專利許可證的國家。十九世紀初期，黏膠是由骨頭、橡膠、合成材料、石油產品等所製成。工業革命和世界大戰加速了黏膠科技的發展，不久之後，黏膠就開始由合成的化合物如酚醛樹脂所製成。現代科技已幾乎不需使用到任何動物副產品來製作黏膠。化學黏膠既持久、有更好的黏著力，又能承受各種極端的溫度和壓力。今日，大多數舊式黏膠已經被合成化合物所取代。

　　有趣的是，雖然黏膠的重大發展和對它的研究直到最近一百年才開始，黏膠在六千年前就已被使用。黏膠已經成為人類生活中不可或缺的必需品了。

解析

1. 本篇依年代敘述黏膠的歷史，黏膠在各年代有不同的發明人以及特殊的用途，所以全篇的大意仍著重在黏膠的發展史，故選(D)黏膠的歷史。

2. 本題考文章細節。第二段中提到羅馬人用魚膠，而之前的巴比倫人及埃及人都用獸皮膠，故答案選(B)獸皮。

3. 本題考文章細節。由最後一段 glues were available 6,000 years ago 可得知黏膠在六千年前就已被使用，故選(A)。

4. 本題考文章理解。由第四段 Industrial production of glue started in Holland 知道(B)是錯的，因為第一家黏膠工廠是設在荷蘭而非英國，故選(B)。

5. 由關鍵字後一句得知黏膠一開始用來修補器皿，所以可由黏膠的黏性推至 sticky 一字，故選(C)。

---

bond　vi.　黏合　　　patent　n.　專利；專利證書　　　phenolic resin　n.　酚醛樹脂

翻譯

　　十八世紀以降，世界上大概沒有比愛爾蘭作家強納森・斯威夫特還偉大且敏銳的諷刺作家了。在他著名的《格列佛遊記》一書中，斯威夫特批判並試圖教育人類大眾。他想要讓人類明白自己的缺點並進而革除它們。若斯威夫特現在還活著，他不知道會有多驚駭，因為在過去兩百年間，人類還是沒有太大改變。

　　斯威夫特在故事中創造出一種名為包伯丁納吉恩的巨人族。他們的一切和生活的社會都巨大無比，身上的毛孔、排泄物以及困擾著他們的蟲子全都巨大而噁心。因為格列佛比巨人族人小太多，他被迫專注在他們所忽略的「小」事物上。斯威夫特利用這些巨人來批判人類社會總習慣去避免生命中那些似乎很瑣碎、令人不愉快但卻十分重要的事物。悲哀的是，人類如今還是繼續忽略著世界上大家都不想要，但確實值得我們注意的事物。

　　媒體和我們這些忠實觀眾往往會忽略掉比當天頭條新聞還大的事件。例如，曾經有個名人就因為被控虐待兒童而成為媒體焦點。但幾乎沒有任何新聞報導烏干達所發生的人道慘劇——反抗軍的逼迫使人民活活餓死。我們像巨人族的本性也在這時顯現：當關於伊拉克戰爭的報導篇幅遠超過在伊朗造成一萬五千人死亡的地震的報導篇幅，不過幸好，在伊拉克戰爭中的死亡人數無法和伊朗地震的死亡人數相比。類似的例子不勝枚舉。我們把在北韓的飢荒問題、在盧安達發生的大屠殺、在非洲不可勝數的愛滋病患者，都掃到良知以外的角落視若無睹。我們會減少對可怖新聞報導的注意力，這點很自然，因為那些新聞駭人到不堪想像，

或者離我們自身的現實生活太遙遠，然而，如果我們不去注意這些可怕的災難事件，又如何能幫助那些急需協助的人？有數百萬人正倚賴我們公平而允當地判斷出事情孰輕孰重。對於這些人來說，我們都不該再繼續當個巨人族的人了。

解析

1. 文中第二段提到當時的人習於忽略似乎細微，實際上卻重要的事物，而可悲的是，當今的人依然有類似的缺點，故意對值得注意卻不討喜的事情視而不見。第三段接著舉例說明。所以本文的目的是(D)提醒大家多注意生活中真正重要的事。

2. 文章第二段描述的包伯丁納吉恩是巨人族，所以(B)的 miniature「袖珍的」是錯誤的用字；(A)(D)文內沒有提到；(C)提到那裡的昆蟲也很巨大，的確「非正常體型」為對，故選(C)。

3. 根據第三段可知伊朗地震有一萬五千人喪生，「好在」伊拉克戰爭沒死這麼多人；只是後者報導的篇幅大於前者，故選(B)少於一萬五千人。

4. 第三段表示人們不關注一些駭人聽聞的新聞報導，因為太令人難受或者距離太過遙遠。而(D)要大家關注由人為疏失引起的事件而非天災，但文章並無此意，故選(C)。

5. 由第一段可知過去二百年來，這樣的情況並沒有多少改善，可見如果斯威夫特現在還在世，可能會相當「驚訝」，故選(A)震驚的。

---

satirist　n.　諷刺作家　　　human race　n.　人類　　　excrement　n.　排泄物　　　occurrence　n.　事件

patronize　vt.　資助；光顧　　　calamity　n.　災難　　　dire　adj.　急迫的

翻譯

城市是大而擁擠，充滿噪音和污染的地方。它忙碌的生活方式會逐漸耗損人的精神和體力。城市居民們太埋首於自己的生活和行事計畫中，使他們幾乎很少跟周圍的其他人互動。即使在眾多人群和娛樂活動的包圍之下，他們仍會感到無比寂寞。因此，許多身陷永無休止的競爭中的城市居民，時常夢想能在鄉間過著更簡單而輕鬆的生活。

從城市搬到鄉間的人，需要在生活上做出很大的調整。城市雖然令人目眩神迷，卻也提供了許多選擇和便利設施。而在鄉間，不再有許多餐廳或店鋪可供選擇，也許只有一兩個小地方可以買到食物，7–11 便利商店則可能要開三十分鐘的車才會到。並且，開車幾乎是唯一的交通方式，而不像大部分的城市裡有巴士、地鐵或渡船可以選擇。若要辦理一些官方或政府事務如駕照登記或選民註冊等，則還是要回到城市或至少較大一點的鎮上才能處理。

然而，在鄉間生活雖然失去了這些便利性，卻也有許多其他好處。在鄉間空氣和水必定更為清新乾淨，交通也順暢許多，停車也絕對不再是個問題。人們一般說來更為放鬆和親切，孩子也能在一個更自由、安全及平和的環境中成長。比起住在毫無特色又獨善其身的城市，住在小鎮的年長者往往和家庭、朋友及土地有更密切的聯繫。

從一個擁擠、狂亂的環境轉換到一個開放而放鬆的環境中也許不難，但從一個忙碌、以自我為中心而且物質化的生活方式，轉換到一個步調較慢、較群體導向的生活方式，難度就可能高得多。大多數人就無法適應這種轉變，很快就回到刺激、便利，讓他們有安全感的城市生活模式中。然而有些人能夠成功地轉換過來，使他們自己和家人都獲益。這些少數人，確實讓他們的夢想成真了。

解析

1. 本篇主要談及城裡人雖嚮往鄉居生活，卻難適應單調不方便的鄉村生活，故選(C)城裡人很難適應鄉村生活。(A)無法忍受都會生活的忙碌或是(B)鄉居生活的無聊均只是文章中的細節；作者強調適應問題的現實面，文中並未提及(D)都會人須搬家至鄉下的必要性。

2. 根據第一段 City people are so wrapped up in their own lives and schedules that they hardly interact with their fellow citizens 可知都會人傾向於孤立自己，故選(A)。他們常嚮往簡單、放鬆的鄉居生活，由第一段最後一句可知(B)(C)不對，文中並未提及(D)。

3. (A)指都會生活的缺點。由第一段最後一句可知(B)(C)都指鄉居生活的優點，跟城市生活無關。從第二段敘述的鄉居生活各項不便，可推論都會生活的最大好處在於便利性及交通的便捷，故選(D)。

4. 由最後一段 Most are unable to make such a transition and return soon to the...city routine 可知(B)大部分的都會人不能適應簡單、緩慢步調的鄉居生活。文中並未提及(A)(C)(D)的敘述。

5. 第一段敘述都會人的忙碌、擁擠、孤獨的生活。可推測 rat race 指都會人如滾輪中的老鼠般無目的地盲目瞎忙，所以選(A)。文中並未談到老鼠，故(B)(C)(D)選項不對。

---

hectic adj. 忙亂的　　ferry n. 渡輪　　registration n. 登記　　attachment n. 情感
anonymous adj. 無特色的　　frantic adj. 狂亂的

翻譯

　　1885 年，馬克吐溫的小說《頑童歷險記》首度出版，內容講述一名叛逆的青少年跟一個名叫吉姆的逃跑奴隸乘坐木筏，順著密西西比河而下一路旅行的故事。這本書使馬克吐溫成為家喻戶曉的名字，該書如今也被視為典型的美國作品。偉大的美國小說家海明威曾表示：「所有現代美國文學都始自一本書，那就是馬克吐溫的《頑童歷險記》。」是什麼特質使《頑童歷險記》成為如此獨特的美國小說？

　　其中一項重要因素在於馬克吐溫使用美式俚語和片語寫作。在馬克吐溫之前，很少美國作家以特別美式的語言創作。他們大多模仿英國作家的優雅對話風格，因為當時的觀念認為偉大的文學不應該包含普通人使用的粗俗語言。然而，馬克吐溫希望讀者能認同他書中的角色們和他們的說話方式。書中的敘事者哈克是個未受教育的孩子，滿口操著不合文法的英語。例如，當他提到曾有一名女子教過他聖經時，他說：「她學我」，而不是「她教我」。他也用一些口語化的字如「我可不」，而非「我不」，此外也常用「他不」、「你不」等字眼。吉姆黑人式英語中也充滿俚語，今日的讀者有時可能會難以理解吉姆說的話。

　　以自由為主題是另一項使這本小說有種獨特美式韻味的因素。吉姆想要逃離自己的奴隸生活，而哈克想幫助他。起初哈克不確定自己這麼做對不對，但當吉姆變成他的朋友之後，他就確定這麼做是對的。很明顯地，馬克吐溫刻意要揭露出種族歧視的態度以及奴隸制度的不公。這本小說同時也處理到另一種層次的自由——漫遊的自由。當哈克沒有預設特定目的地，就這麼順著密西西比河而下的時候，他已擺脫了社會規範，這種自由的概念影響了日後的美國文學。

解析

1. 第一段段末問了「什麼因素使《頑童歷險記》成為有美國特色的小說？」接著第二、三段提出答案說明，故選(A)。(B)不正確，因為本篇主題重點並非在討論這本小說對現代美國文學的影響。

2. 第三段提到馬克吐溫要顯露當時種族歧視的態度和奴隸制度的不公平。第三段開頭和結尾也各自提到「自由」的可貴，故答案為(D)。至於(C)，雖然第二段有提到馬克吐溫希望讀者能認同他書中的人物，以及他們說話的方式。但是(C)不夠明確，若改成「介紹馬克吐溫那個時代一般美國人的語言」較為正確。

3. 本題考文章細節。第二段提到吉姆黑人式英語充滿俚語，現代讀者有時會覺得他的話難以理解，故選(B)。

4. 本題考文章推理。由第二段可知馬克吐溫那個時代的美國作家多數模仿英國作家「典雅」的對話，故推論「頑童歷險記」可能在當時並不受推崇，所以選(D)。(A)不對，馬克吐溫並沒有贊成種族主義和奴隸制度；(B)(C)無法推知。

5. 由第二段得知因為當時認為偉大的文學不應含有一般人使用的粗俗語言 (coarse language)，故選(C)通俗的，粗俗的。此字延續前題 / 句，與 elegant 為相反詞。

runaway adj. 逃跑的　　ungrammatical adj. 不合文法的　　grasp vt. 理解

O9 真心誠意
Being All Heart

翻譯

這項消息本來不該令她訝異，全國每個人都知道這件事終究會發生。但那仍然令人震驚：他們竟然殺了她丈夫。

當班尼格諾在 1983 年被謀殺時，柯拉蓉・艾奎諾 (這個名字在西班牙文中是「心」的意思) 正好嫁給他 29 年。他是菲律賓獨裁者馬可仕的頭號政敵。多年來，班尼格諾一直在國內鼓吹民主自由，也因此使他和他的家人被放逐到美國。雖然大家都警告他，一旦他回到祖國馬可仕一定會除掉他，但他仍堅持返國。他的死使他立刻成為一名烈士，並促使柯拉蓉成為一場革命的領導者。

原本是一名平凡家庭主婦的柯拉蓉一點都不想成為政治英雄。但她知道受打壓的人民需要她，而菲律賓必須有所改變。她的心無法不響應同胞們對公平正義的要求，於是柯拉蓉加入總統選舉，成為馬可仕的競爭對手。雖然馬可仕自行宣布勝選，但大家都很清楚是柯拉蓉獲得大多數的選票。選舉結果被操縱了，成千上萬的民眾湧上街頭抗議數天之久。馬可仕明白自己已經落敗，於是離開菲律賓，從此未再返國，一場成功且平和的民眾力量革命圓滿落幕，而若非柯拉蓉決定接受領導者的職位，這場革命就不可能發生。

身為新總統的柯拉蓉持續廉正執政，並在最需要的地方做改變。她恢復國家的媒體自由，進行憲法改革，使馬可仕那樣的獨裁者不會再有機會掌權，並使動盪不安的菲律賓南部保持和平。最重要的是，她帶給菲律賓人希望，因為一名普通人也可以用正直、誠意以及正義感治理國家。直到現在，無論何時她以退休政治人物的身份出現在公眾場合，她閃耀的個人魅力都會使群眾大喊她的暱稱「柯蕊！柯蕊！」。無疑地，柯拉蓉・艾奎諾是真心誠意的。

解析

1. 全篇主旨敘述柯拉蓉・艾奎諾當菲律賓總統的前因後果，故選(D)柯拉蓉・艾奎諾如何當上菲律賓總統的過程。(A)目前菲律賓的政治現況並未提及；全文非單指(B)某一女政治家從小到老的自傳；(C)菲律賓如何成為一個民主國家的過程並未在本文概述其始末。

2. 由第三段得知柯拉蓉・艾奎諾原是平凡的家庭主婦，先生被暗殺後，了解被壓迫的 (oppressed) 人民需要她，感受到同胞們 (compatriots) 渴求公正，她才決定參選總統，故選(C)。她並非(A)單想報復對手，或是(B)証明自己的能力，(D)亦不對，大家已知兇手，所以她參選的目的並非找出殺夫兇手。

3. 由第三段 The elections were **rigged** 得知選舉是不公平的，故選(B)。

4. 本題考文章細節，由末段可知因為柯拉蓉的憲法改革使得馬可仕沒有機會再掌權，故選(C)柯拉蓉・艾奎諾使馬可仕不能再當總統。文中第三段僅提到馬可仕離開菲律賓，未再返國，但並未述及(A)被流放美國；(B)不對，民眾力量革命是柯拉蓉・艾奎諾所領導而非馬可仕；文中未提及(D)柯拉蓉・艾奎諾操作媒體。

5. 柯拉蓉・艾奎諾的先生被馬可仕害死，反而讓她先生變成烈士；本字後面的 **propelled** 含正向線索，故選(A)。

---

dictator　n.　獨裁者　　exile　vt.　流放　　compatriot　n.　同胞　　rig　vt.　(用不正當手段) 操縱

tyrant　n.　專制君主　　decency　n.　正派　　charisma　n.　魅力

10 照相機：攝影界的明星
The Camera: the Star of Shooting

翻譯

　　一切始於 1839 年，赫瑟爾爵士首先使用「攝影」這個字來解釋他用光捕捉一個世間景像的實驗。「攝影 (photography)」是一個希臘字，意指用光作畫，所以早期的照片常被稱為「光畫」。「光畫」最神奇的地方在於，只要有正確的工具，任何人都能創作出一幅來，而這項工具就是照相機！

　　然而，要發展出可使用的照相機卻是項困難的任務。最早的大眾用照相機是達蓋爾所發明，但他花了十二年時間才發明出一種可以產生相片的機器。當達蓋爾那台名為達蓋爾型的新相機在 1839 年對大眾發售時，「無須任何繪畫知識」的廣告詞使它一夕成名。

　　不過，早期的相片完全不像今日這種幾秒內就可產生的數位影像。達蓋爾的照相機本身是個木盒子，一頭是鏡片，另一頭則是要放進金屬照片盤的溝槽。整體結構並不複雜，但拍照過程很困難，需要小心謹慎才能正確地捕捉影像。整個過程很費時，最初的照片也龐大而笨重，此外費用也是一項重要考量。因此，只有錢人才能負擔得起這種保存重要場合影像的方式，或藉由被拍成人像照片而變得不朽。

　　照相機的新發明以及照相過程的改進則改變了這一切。沒多久，每個人就都能負擔得起照張人像照片，如今相片更成為現代生活中非常重要的一部份。照相機科技的演進，讓我們能看到世界另一邊的人和地方的樣子。我們可以記錄歷史事件，把自己心肝寶貝的照片放在口袋裡，看著月球表面，或一窺人體內部。今日，家族合照以及塞滿相片的相簿在世界各地的家庭中都非常常見。

解析

1. 由第一段提到「照相」指的是「用光作畫」，故本題答案為 (B) 光線。

2. 本題考文章推理。第二段提及達蓋爾花了十二年發明照相機，而段末提到 1839 年他的照相機公諸於世，所以倒推回去，他從 1827 年開始發明，故選 (D)。

3. 根據第二段最後一句得知使用此照相機不需繪畫的知識，因此使其立即受到歡迎，故選 (B)。

4. 由第三段的 **time-consuming** 可知照相的過程很費時，可推論日後的改善有部份著重於縮短其耗費的時間，故選 (A)。(B) 不對，赫瑟爾爵士只是首先使用「攝影」的人；(C)(D) 無法推知。

5. 第三段最後一句提到只有富人才有錢透過照片保存特別的活動，或使自己「不朽」；因為透過照片記下生活片刻，當下的精彩便因照片每次看到每次回味而被永遠記得，故選 (C)；讀者可將四個選項套入原文，找出合理的答案。(A) 珍貴的；(B) 永遠活著；(D) 舉國著稱。

slot　n.　狹長孔　　　bulky　adj.　龐大的

翻譯

即使在今日，還是令人很難相信比薩斜塔這座五十六公尺高的八層樓建築物，能以比正常垂直軸偏斜約十度的狀態傾斜地屹立超過八百年之久。

比薩是義大利中世紀時期的主要權力中心，居民們想要蓋一座全歐洲最高的鐘塔來展顯他們的力量。1173 年，建築工程在建築師博南諾・皮薩諾的監督下開始。不久之後被迫停工，因為他們發現塔開始往北傾斜。博南諾害怕同胞們的怒火，於是逃到國外了。

幾近一世紀之後，建築師試圖以慢慢把它往反方向推的方式重新改建這座塔，但因比薩陷入戰爭中使得工程再遭擱置。最後終於在 1350 年，博南諾的親戚托馬索・皮薩諾在塔傾斜的狀態下將它完成，方法是在第七層樓南側的突出飛簷部分往上再加兩個階梯。完工時，這座塔被視為近代世界的奇觀。

至今它仍然是個奇觀。八百年來它從來沒有停止傾斜。這座塔一直穩定地以每年五角秒 (約 1.2 公釐) 的速度傾斜中。有好幾世紀之久，人們以為傾斜是因為設計上的瑕疵使然，現在科學家們發現問題在於土壤。這座塔豎立在原本是港灣的流動沙土上，土壤中缺乏足以支撐如此巨大建築物的力量。

1934 年，義大利將軍墨索里尼下令在地基加入幾乎兩百噸的水泥，想藉此把塔弄直，結果反而造成嚴重危機。在 1990 年代，巨大的鐘不再鳴響，入塔的樓梯不再對大眾開放。然而在 1995 年，比薩政府為了準備在塔內植入一個隱藏的電纜系統，開始以液化氮冷凍地面，但此舉幾乎使整個塔被連根拔起。塔開始以每天四角秒 (約一公釐) 的危險速度往南傾斜。

終於在 1998 年末，他們決定採用替換土壤的方法，將位於北側的軟質泥土慢慢地挖出來並替換掉。

解析

1. 本文敘述比薩斜塔的建造過程，比薩斜塔的建造歷史最符合文章大意，故選(C)。(A)(B)(D)僅述及其中片段細節。
2. 根據第一段，比薩斜塔的傾斜狀態已超過八百年，一直被認為是奇蹟，故選(A)。(B)它建造於軟泥上是後來科學家的發現；(C)建一座全歐最高鐘塔來宣揚國威是義大利建造比薩鐘塔的原意。
3. 由第四段 Now scientists have discovered that the problems lie in the **soil** 得知答案為(C)。
4. 見本文的最末句，抽換塔下的泥土才是根本的解決之道，故選(D)。
5. 關鍵字前面的 **fearing** 以及句末的 **went into exile** (流放他國)，加上前句描述的發現北邊傾斜，立即停工，可推測本字字義為(B)憤怒。

axis n. 軸線   tilt n. 傾斜   cornice n. 飛簷   shift vi./vt. 移動   estuary n. 河口
nitrogen n. 氮

翻譯

　　想像一下：你身在一個桶子中被拖進尼加拉河。現在你以每小時一百公里的速度移動，「砰」地撞過急流中的石頭。接著你抵達瀑布邊緣，而後垂直墜下 52 公尺。當你抵達瀑布底部時，是以時速 350 公里的速度撞上水面。你帶著足以粉身碎骨的衝力撞上去，這對身體的衝擊簡直難以言喻。如今你大概已經失去意識了——如果你還沒死的話。如此一來，你就成了尼加拉大瀑布著名的敢死隊之一。

　　尼加拉河流經伊利湖和安大略湖之間，形成美國紐約州和加拿大安大略省之間的部分國界。河上有一連串壯觀的瀑布，而尼加拉大瀑布是世界上最大的瀑布之一。想像每秒鐘有三千噸的水流下瀑布，這可是足以壓垮任何生物的重量。

　　最早的敢死隊成員是走鋼索表演者，其中最著名的是「偉大布朗丁」，他在 19 世紀中期拉起一條橫跨這座瀑布的鋼索，並矇著眼睛走過去，他也曾騎腳踏車通過這條鋼索。

　　一直到 1901 年才有人把自己裝在木桶裡翻落瀑布。數年來，一共有十六人在木桶中翻落瀑布，其中六人在過程中死亡。1993 年，一名叫做大衛・墨菲的加拿大人是最後一個嘗試這項舉動的人。在那之後，因為這項舉動實在太過危險，加拿大和美國政府都禁止任何人再翻落瀑布。除此之外，這項冒險之舉也可能對瀑布造成傷害，因為瀑布上的石頭又軟又易碎。如今這種驚險表演是違法的，而且可能被科以美金一萬元的罰金。

解析

1. 第一段第一句要讀者想像自己在一個桶子裡被丟進尼加拉河中。接下來整段描述從瀑布墜下的驚險歷程，故選(A)引起讀者自行想像一段刺激旅程。

2. 本題考文章推理。第四段前兩句提到 1901 年至 1993 年有 16 人前往挑戰，其中 6 人死亡。故選(C) 10 人倖存。

3. 本題考文章細節。由第四段段末 The stunts are now illegal and can result in a fine of US$ 10,000 得知此舉不但違法，而且可能要被罰鍰，故選(A)。

4. 第一段提及猛烈撞擊急流中的大岩石，又提到撞擊水面的力量是粉身碎骨的力道，還有對身體驚人的衝擊，以上兩處均顯示對冒險者構成威脅，故選(D)。此外，雖然第四段提到美、加政府都禁止在尼加拉瀑布從事冒險行徑，但不表示沒有人將會繼續嘗試，故(A)不正確。文章亦無法看出(B)失敗的冒險者都被淹死，或是(C)走繩索橫越尼加拉瀑布比較勇敢。

5. 第一段可以看出這些 daredevil「膽大包天的人」做的事極其危險，故選(B)。

---

slam　vi. 猛擊　　　unconscious　adj. 不省人事的，失去知覺的　　　tightrope　n. 鋼索

blindfolded　adv. 眼睛被遮住地

翻譯

　　為了贏得五萬元美金，你願意做什麼？例如，你願意從摩天大樓樓頂高空彈跳嗎？還是喝下老鼠湯──將六種老鼠攪成泥狀的東西？為了這筆錢，你會願意把頭塞進一個放滿蛇的玻璃箱子裡嗎？如果你敢，那你不是唯一的一個。許多人在實境電視秀裡做過更可怕的事，還有上百萬人會看著你通過這些絕不造假而令人心驚膽戰的挑戰。

　　實境電視秀是理應沒有劇本的電視秀。實境電視節目裡演出的不是演員，而是就像你我的普通人。它們不會像肥皂劇或警探影集一樣講些虛構故事，而是展現出平常人面臨到極端狀況時的反應。實境電視秀裡的人們所感受、所做的決定和說出的話都是發自內心，並且會導致實際的後果。

　　1948 年首度開播的《隱藏攝影機》被認為是所有實境電視秀的先驅，而真正有所突破的則是 MTV 台所播出的《真實世界》。在這部至今已經播出 15 年的電視秀裡，會有七個人住進同一間屋子裡，他們的一切行動會透過攝影機呈現出來，長達 2000 小時之久。觀眾能親眼目睹這些人如何對他人使壞或展現仁慈。《我要活下去》系列可能是最多人收看的實境電視秀，節目中有十八個人身處在一個異國地點如澳洲內陸，並且必須在一面忍受原始環境和面對無數挑戰的情況下，一面使自己比其他人存活得更久。每週都會透過投票淘汰一名競爭者，直到最後只剩下獲勝的「唯一生存者」，獨得一百萬美元獎金。

　　實境電視秀有時會在許多方面影響到人們的生活。例如，在《交換妻子》及《互換配偶》中，來自非常不同生活背景的兩對夫婦互換生活地點。每對夫婦必須和一個陌生的家庭相處，而最後，兩邊的夫婦都會對自己和他人有些新的認知。參加者在現場會暴露出人類真實的天性，並讓觀眾思考，若自己身處在他們的情況下又會怎麼做。對於實境電視秀的製作者、參加者以及觀眾而言，真相無疑是唯一重要的事。

解析

1. 由第二段 They show how ordinary people react when they are put in extraordinary situations 可知答案為(B)。

2. 第三段指出《隱藏攝影機》是所有實境電視秀的先驅，接著可推算 **2009–1948=61**；因此，至今已超過五十年，故選(C)。(D)不對，邁向第十五個年頭的是《真實世界》，它只是所有實境秀之一，不是實境秀出現至今的時間。

3. 本題考文章細節。由第三段中間的 The *Survivor* series may be the most watched programs 可知答案是(C)。

4. 本文從第一段至第三段均提到實境秀令觀眾為之瘋狂的情況，並都有提到勝利者有豐厚的獎金，故選(A)人們會為了一筆為數可觀的獎金做任何事。本文不但顯示(B)人性中的自私自利，還有貪婪、冒險犯難等；(C)也不對，雖然不全是黑暗面，也絕對不全是光明面；(D)在文中沒有提到。

5. outlast each other 指在競賽中，須打敗對方，故選(D)，讀者可由關鍵字後描述每週淘汰一名參賽者直到最後一位冠軍勝出的情況推測答案。fight for 指「為某人或某目的而戰」。

---

stew n. 燉煮的菜肴　　authentic adj. 真實的　　nerve-racking adj. 極使人不安的
precursor n. 始祖

翻譯

　　西班牙在十九世紀是一股龐大的殖民勢力，其帝國範圍遍佈全球，在非洲、亞洲以及大部分中南美洲都有殖民地。但到了 1898 年，由於美洲一些地區獨立革命成功，西班牙帝國縮減到剩下加勒比海的古巴和波多黎各群島及太平洋的關島和菲律賓。在同一年，由於一名美國人的影響，西班牙帝國全面垮台。這個人就是美國報業大亨威廉‧魯道夫‧赫斯特。

　　出生富裕家庭的赫斯特，年僅 23 歲時就開始收購報社。七年後，他在美國所有主要都市擁有一連串的雜誌社和報社，使他在散播資訊上擁有極大影響力。就某方面說來他是成功的，因為他雇用許多有名作家，並且率先在自己的出版品上使用彩色印刷。透過他的報社，赫斯特的影響力大到能使一個帝國倒台。

　　赫斯特和西班牙政府在土地所有權上展開論戰，並挑起一股對西班牙的強烈敵意。他利用自己的報紙譴責西班牙人既落後、腐敗又壓迫他人，此外亦鼓勵支持古巴和菲律賓的獨立運動。赫斯特的影響力如此之大，以致於當古巴和菲律賓的革命爆發時，他立即說服美國人民在 1898 年對西班牙宣戰。隨之而來的戰爭由美國獲勝，西班牙帝國終於宣告結束。關島和波多黎各歸屬於美國，而古巴和菲律賓則成為獨立國家。

　　媒體在型塑公眾意見和影響事件走向上的力量有多龐大這方面，赫斯特是一個重要例證。

解析

1. 由第一段最後一句可知西班牙帝國的瓦解完全是由於美國報業鉅子赫斯特的影響，其後段落皆描述他使西班牙帝國垮台的前因後果，故選(D)赫斯特的影響力。

2. 文中第二段提到赫斯特是首位在出版物裡使用彩色印刷的人，這可算是一大突破，故選(C)。

3. 第三段提到 1898 年赫斯特遊說美國人民對西班牙宣戰，這場戰爭美國獲勝，西班牙帝國失敗，故選(B)。

4. 赫斯特是利用他辦報紙所產生的輿論力量影響美國人仇視西班牙帝國，因此不但支持其殖民地的獨立，還進而發動戰爭使其潰敗滅亡，故(C)文筆的力量勝過刀劍這句話最能總結本文的主旨。其它選項(A)驕者必敗；(B)我們都是輿論之奴，受其牽制；(D)團結則立；分歧則亡皆不適合。

5. 由關鍵字後的 **backward**、**corrupt**、**oppressive** 等負面用詞，推斷(A)公開嚴厲地批評為答案。

---

leverage　n.　影響力　　acquire　vt.　獲得　　a string of　一連串的　　backward　adj.　落後的
cede　vt.　割讓　　mold　vt.　對…產生影響

15 陷入危機的觀光景點
Tourist Destination in Danger

翻譯

　　從遠處看，它就像漂浮在一大片藍色背景中的閃亮珠寶。這座自每本印度觀光小冊子和導覽書上躍然而出的白色大理石建築，它的美麗和壯觀必定令你嘆為觀止。

　　除了是一座建築奇蹟之外，泰姬瑪哈陵背後迷人的羅曼史使今日的觀光客不願意錯過這個地方。陵寢本身是真愛的例證，一位蒙兀兒君王在 1653 年建造這座陵墓，作為他的愛妻永恆安息之地。到現在，它仍然在觀光客心中注入一種溫柔的愛情感受，而這點某方面來說為它帶來了災難。

　　每年有大批觀光客前來造訪泰姬瑪哈陵，旺季時一天的遊客數更高達到驚人的百萬人次。過度暴露使這個珍貴的地方變得脆弱，容易受到損傷。觀光客不只踐踏在細緻的大理石結構上，也帶來龐大垃圾量污染了周圍地區。有些缺乏公德心的觀光客甚至以在大理石上刻下名字的方式宣稱自己的愛。尤有甚者，許多來來去去的公車和三輪計程機車所排出的廢氣、香菸的煙都在侵蝕大理石。一點一點地，大理石正在失去原有的光澤。

　　隨著旅館數目增加，阿格拉這個小鎮也開始往外圍不斷擴張。過度使用水資源再加上設備不足的污水處理系統導致土壤失去水分，這就是為何大理石表面正以令人擔憂的速度出現如頭髮般的細小裂紋。

　　旅行能使心靈開闊，讓人可以親身體驗世界。但是我們必須謹記，爆炸性的觀光業成長，最終卻可能會毀滅掉我們所珍惜的遺產和自然──一旦被毀壞，就無法再復原的資產。

解析

1. 由最後一段 explosive growth of tourism may eventually destroy our treasured heritage and nature 推得本文的重點為(B)旅遊業正摧毀泰姬瑪哈陵。
2. 根據第二段得知泰姬瑪哈陵建於 1653 年，可推算：2009–1653＝355，故選(C)。
3. 由第三段可知遊覽車帶來的觀光客、觀光客抽的菸以及車輛廢氣等全都是損害古蹟的原因，故選(D)以上皆是。
4. (B)(C)(D)在第三段都可找到，本文並未提及政府對這一切狀況所做的措施，故選(A)。
5. 第三段都在陳述觀光業對於古蹟的損害；而由關鍵字後描述觀光客在石頭上刻字的行為，可推知答案為(D)欠缺思考的。

stretch　n.　延亙，連綿　　onlooker　n.　旁觀者　　overexposure　n.　過度暴露　　rickshaw　n.　人力車
sewage　n.　污水

翻譯

雪上滑板到底是什麼？對某些人來說，它是一種生活方式。對其他人來說，它是一種在斜坡上進行的冬季運動之一，而且讓許多從事滑雪運動者心生疑慮，不知自己是否不久就要落伍了。玩雪上滑板需要用到一塊滑板，玩家的兩隻腳會被綁在上面，乘著滑板一面滑下山坡，一面以跟滑雪者類似的方式運用身體重量做出一連串扭身和轉體動作。

許多人將雪上滑板視為相對來說較現代的運動，是由一些想在冬天也能玩滑板的青少年發明並普及化。不過，雪上滑板的歷史可追溯至 1929 年，第一個類似雪板的物件在那時被製造出來。

第一塊「雪板」是一個名叫傑克·布區特的人所發明。為了能滑下斜坡，他試圖用曬衣繩將一塊三夾板固定在雙腳上。這個初步的模型被使用超過三十年後才有下一項突破產生。1965 年，「雪上衝浪者」被發明出來，那是一塊單片像雪橇的板子，前端連著一條繩子用來控制方向。

自此之後，雪板歷經許多改革，包括加上綑綁器。這個裝置一方面取代了方向控制繩，另一方面能固定玩家的腳。板子的形狀也有所改變，看起來頗像壓扁的雪茄，使它們更符合空氣動力學。雖然在雪上滑板的概念出現至今已過近 80 年，直到最近 10 到 15 年間，這項運動才真正在冬季運動愛好者中居於主導地位。

這項運動真正躋身主流是在 1998 年，雪上滑板運動在當年的冬季奧運中首度正式在世人面前亮相，自此之後，這項運動就變得越來越受歡迎。雖然今日許多滑雪者不喜歡和雪上滑板運動者共用滑雪坡，但在世界各地的滑雪勝地已經時常可以看到雪上滑板運動者的身影。如今，它受歡迎的程度更甚以往，每年有超過五百萬名雪上滑板運動者在雪坡上大顯身手，看來，雪上滑板運動已有自己的一片天而且不打算離開雪地了。

解析

1. 本篇前兩段主要在介紹雪上滑板，後三段主要講其從發明到目前風行的情形，故選(C)雪上滑板的發展。(A)(B)只是文內的細節；(D)文中沒有提到。

2. 很多滑雪的人懷疑「自己是否不久就要落伍了 (be part of the history)」，這意味著滑雪可能會被雪上滑板所取代，故選(D)。至於(A)滑雪者將名留青史；(B)滑雪運動影響運動史；(C)滑雪者創下重要紀錄皆非正解。

3. 雪上滑板需有滑雪斜坡、滑雪板之外，文章在第四段提及...the attachment of bindings, which replace the rope and are used to secure a rider，可見方向控制繩非必要配備，故選(B)。

4. 第五段提到雪上滑板在 1998 年成為冬季奧運會的項目，從此越來越風行，故選(B)。

5. 第四段提到滑雪板的形狀和以往不同，多數像扁平的雪茄，為的是讓板子「更符合空氣動力學 (= 更流線型 = 速度更快)」，故選(A)。其它選項套入上下文，皆無法產生適當語意。

---

strap　vt.　用帶子捆綁住…　　　plywood　n.　三夾板　　　clothesline　n.　曬衣繩　　　downhill　adv.　向坡下
steer　vt.　操縱　　　devotee　n.　愛好者　　　be here to stay　phr.　被接受並被廣泛使用

17 奈米小巨人
The Small Giant

翻譯

　　奈米科技能在醫藥領域創造奇蹟，它在一個由電腦控制的環境下跟原子——萬物的最小單位——共同合作。想像一下，一隊比人類細胞還小的分子工具進入你的身體，為你奮戰並保護你不受細菌製造大軍所造成的損害和崩解之害。這些被恰如其分地命名為奈米機器人的奈米機器，會在人的身體裡自由循環流動，判定被感染的區域並用細膩而精確的方式摧毀之，而你根本感覺不到自己身體裡正發生的活動。而且，你只需要吞下一顆小膠囊，或忍受一下不太痛的針刺就好了。

　　就像機器人一樣，奈米機器人什麼都能做。它們能在你得心血管疾病之前就幫你把動脈中的膽固醇清除；能殺死那些有時連最詳盡的健康檢查都測不出來的癌細胞，或其他危及生命的病毒。從此我們不再需要經歷痛苦的手術——因為這些小小軍隊會治癒並修復任何未正常運作的器官。此外也不需要接受痛苦的牙科治療，因為簡單的奈米機器輕易地就能解決這個問題。

　　然而，奈米科技最大的益處在於它能抵達受感染的確切地點，因此能降低副作用。若沒有奈米科技，每年約有十萬人死於副作用的影響。

　　科學家預測，上述各點在未來三十年間大多都能夠達成。雖然這項主張一直被取笑，但也不可能完全是天方夜譚。不久之後，一個充滿驚奇和奇蹟，令我們瞠目結舌的時代就要展開了。

解析

1. 全篇從第一段的主題句 Nanotechnology can create wonders in the fields of medicine 開始，接下來的兩段均在討論奈米科技在醫藥上的運用。末段除了總結其神妙功能 (曾被嘲笑不可能) 之外，更預測將來還有更令人瞠目結舌的功能，故選(C)奈米科技如何運用在醫學領域。

2. 由第一段末句 all you have to do is swallow an undersized capsule 得知答案為(C)我們可以吞下奈米機器。

3. 因第一段 It works...in a computer-controlled environment 而知道奈米科技是在電腦控制的環境下發揮作用，可知答案為(B)電腦。

4. 由第三段 However, the most useful benefit of nanotechnology is its access to the exact location of infection 推得(A)為答案。(B)為非，奈米機器人是可以殺死連詳盡的健康檢查都沒測到的癌細胞；(C)為非，有了奈米科技，我們就不用經歷痛苦的手術，而不是外科醫生就不能施行手術；(D)每年造成十萬人死亡的是副作用而不是奈米科技的誤用。

5. 關鍵字出現在末段最後一句，因末段總結其曾被嘲笑不可能的神妙功能，可推測將來還有更令人目眩神迷的功能，故選(D)。

---

a fleet of 一隊　　molecular adj. 分子的　　justifiably adv. 正當地　　sting n. 刺痛
cholesterol n. 膽固醇　　artery n. 動脈　　cardiovascular adj. 心血管的　　check-up n. 健康檢查
dysfunctional adj. 不正常的

18 少點噓聲，多些掌聲
Less Boo, More Boost

翻譯

在美國，雇主因為人的外表或缺陷而歧視該人是違法行為。這種概念在 1990 年透過《美國殘障者法案》的頒佈正式立法確立，並為原本幾乎沒有工作機會的人開創出大量機會。

該法案協助勞工的方式之一是要求企業根據殘障者的工作表現而非他們的身體障礙或缺陷來雇用他們。該法案亦透過制訂企業必須遵守的規定準則，使工作地點成為更便於殘障者工作的環境，以確保殘障者在工作場所能得到公平平等的對待。此類規定準則可能包括設置輪椅用斜坡，在電梯內設置點字數字，以及只需按一個按鈕就可開關的門等。

許多因這個法案而帶來的改變如今已變得極為稀鬆平常，使得非殘障人士往往對這個問題並未多加思考。例如很少人知道，商店裡的走道必須夠寬，才能讓輪椅安全地行駛其間。

雖然這項法案讓美國數百萬人受惠，有些企業主卻覺得自己被迫花額外費用更新辦公室，就為了配合一些可能不會進入公司的人，更遑論去應徵的人了。但若企業不依照法案行事，則會因索賠或面對高額罰金而損失更多金錢。

據估計，約有百分之二十的美國人為某種形式的長期殘疾所苦，這意味著這項重要的立法直接嘉惠了約五千萬名美國人。

解析

1. 由第一段和最後一段的頭尾呼應，可以看出本文主旨在談論(C)《美國殘障者法案》如何幫助肢障人士獲得平等的工作權利。(A)(B)(D)皆沒有提及。

2. 根據第二段得知該法案可確保殘障人士在職場得到公平平等的待遇，故選(B)。(A)每家企業要「無條件」雇用殘障人士，但第二段第一句指出是要根據其「工作表現」故不對；(C)殘障人士的薪水比其他員工高文中沒有提及；(D)殘障人士在工作場所不會遇到任何障礙。所謂「障礙」可能包含有形、無形，指涉範圍太廣，因此不適合。

3. 綜合第二段及第三段得知(A)重點不是商店裡「平穩的」走道，而是「寬度可容輪椅通過」的走道，故選(A)。

4. 本題考文章細節。第四段提到若企業不遵守此法案，可能被投訴或面對可觀的罰鍰，故選(D)。因為此法案，所以專為殘障人士設計的設施大家已習以為常，故(A)為非；(B)由第三段得知雖然此法使數千萬人受惠，但是還是有設施有待改進，殘障人士的生活並非從此沒問題；(C)由第四段得知有些企業主不遵守此法案是因為他們認為根本不會有殘障人士進入公司，而非他們效率不高。

5. 由關鍵字後所提的走道的例子，得知該法案所帶來的改善非常司空見慣，所以非殘障人士通常「視其為當然」。所以可代換成(B)不會想到或覺察到。至於(A)不慎重考慮；三思而後行；(C)不同意；(D)不適應，不習慣皆不宜。

---

thereof adv. 其   installation n. 設備   ramp n. 斜坡   venture into 冒險做…   claim n. 索賠
hefty adj. (金額) 龐大的

翻譯

　　能使用乾淨的廁所設施是一項基本人權，但根據世界衛生組織及聯合國環境計畫的調查指出，世界上有超過二十億人只能倚賴跟許多人共用的公共廁所。太多人使用的結果就是使廁所很難保持清潔。疾病從這些廁所快速擴散，每年造成數千人生病甚至死亡。這些驚人的統計數字提醒了我們一個幾乎被遺忘，但全球人都該感到羞愧的情況存在。

　　最缺乏廁所設施的地區是非洲和亞洲。在整個中國，約有百分之五十到七十五的人沒有一個連結到污水處理系統或化糞池的抽水馬桶可用。在印度，恆河岸就是無數人民的廁所，每分鐘有超過一百萬公升未處理的排泄物排入這條河中。世界衛生組織估計，盧安達有百分之九十二的人沒有任何一種廁所設施可使用。太多人共用狹小空間的結果就是很難將食物和廁所污物放置處隔離。

　　由於世界上最貧窮的地區也需要許多其他物資，如食物、醫藥和教育，因此建造適當的廁所設施往往被視為較次要的事務。然而，許多位於富有和貧窮地區的援助組織正共同合作以提供乾淨的廁所給貧窮國家的人使用。在莫三比克，一個當地的援助組織和一個英國組織通力合作改善利欣加鎮的衛生。他們開始用環保廁所取代原始的排泄物坑洞，此種環保廁所只使用非常少的水，並將排泄物和土壤及灰混合製成堆肥。有別於傳統的坑式廁所，這些新式環保廁所聞起來不臭，也不會招來會傳播疾病的蒼蠅或蚊子。更重要的是，只需要花 25 美元就能安裝一座這樣的廁所，而且完全不需要維修。這些環保廁所協助防止疾病擴散，即使是最貧窮國家的人民，這樣的廁所也能改善他們的衛生狀況。

解析

1. 本篇主題是廁所問題。從第一段第一句至文末均談及落後國家的廁所問題，故選(C)。
2. 第二段指出中國約百分之五十到七十五的人家沒有抽水馬桶，而盧安達卻有高達百分之九十二的人家沒有任何廁所設備，故選(B)。
3. 由第一段 Diseases spread quickly from these toilets 得知疾病從不乾淨的廁所快速傳播，故推得答案為(D)。
4. 文中並未提及這些環保廁所類似於坑式廁所，故選(A)。(B)(C)(D)在第三段皆可找到。
5. 從關鍵字出現的文句，以及下面的句子談及生態廁所的推展等可推斷公益團體努力改善當地的衛生情況，故選(B)衛生情況。

---

sewer　n.　污水管　　　septic tank　n.　化糞池　　　Mozambique　莫三比克 (國家名)　　　pit　n.　坑
compost　n.　堆肥

翻譯

　　肺結核和軟骨病這兩種古老的疾病開始重返英國。肺結核這種由細菌引起、有致命可能並會對肺造成嚴重傷害的疾病，在大多數人記憶中是屬於十九世紀的歷史疾病。肺結核應該在 1950 年代就已絕跡，但最近來自英國的醫學資料顯示，自 2000 年到 2006 年間，通報的肺結核病例已達 1790 例。

　　跟肺結核類似，軟骨病也應該已在 1950 年代絕跡，然而，由英國衛生部所進行的研究認為，軟骨病在移民族群的孩童中有百分之一的發病率。軟骨病會因缺乏維他命 D 使骨架彎曲，並而造成孩童的發育障礙。這種古老的疾病若沒有經過適當醫治也可能像肺結核一樣致命。因此，為這兩種疾病的再出現找出原因並加以治療是非常重要的。

　　在這兩種疾病中，移民是共通的因素，儘管在兩種疾病中造成影響的方式不同。具傳染性的肺結核是在患者咳嗽、打噴嚏或說話時經由空氣散播。英國大多數的移民來自亞洲、非洲、加勒比海沿岸國家及中東這些肺結核仍然活躍的地方。不幸的是，從肺結核仍是地方性疾病的國家移民到已開發國家時，這種致命疾病也會跟著可能感染他人的受感染者一起渡海過來。

　　至於軟骨病，來自陽光充足國家的移民會需要較多日照來產生維他命 D，並因此保留製造骨骼的鈣。然而，英國多雲的氣候無法為這些移民提供足夠的日照，而這些移民本身也往往並未意識到自己其實能補充維他命 D 來預防軟骨病。

　　若要預防和杜絕這兩種疾病，英國衛生局對於可能病患的及時注意及有效預防措施是最好的方法。從抗生素、疫苗和有效的肺結核病患管理一起著手，應能將這項疾病從英國根除。同時，英國衛生部也可透過告知移民者應照射充足陽光和定期補充維他命 D 等資訊的方式，協助移民族群預防軟骨病。

解析

1. 由第三段得知肺結核是經由空氣傳染，而第四段指出軟骨病是因為日照不足，使人無法產生足夠的維他命 D 導致，故知(C)兩者皆是主要經由空氣傳播的傳染性疾病為錯。

2. 第二、三、四段分別提到此兩種疾病的起因及症狀；第五段提到治癒的方法。至於死亡率則未提及，故選(D)。

3. 本題考查文章細節。第二段提到軟骨病的病因，故選(B)維他命 D 的缺乏導致骨骼彎曲，孩童發育不良。此外第二段指出軟骨病已在 1950「年代」於英國絕跡，可見(A)不正確；而第四段顯示來自陽光充沛地區的外來移民到英國後容易罹患軟骨病，可見(C)軟骨病為「孩童」特有的「遺傳性」病症不正確；根據第二段提到移民族群中有百分之一孩童患有軟骨病，故(D)百分之一的英國兒童有軟骨病的發病機會不正確。

4. 根據第五段提到抗生素、注射疫苗及有效管理結核病人皆為消除肺結核的對策，故選(A)抗生素。

5. 根據關鍵字前提到肺結核在亞洲、非洲、加勒比海地區及中東仍很活躍，由此可見 endemic 是指某種疾病在某些地區才有的，故選(A)特有且常見。

---

tuberculosis n. 肺結核；結核病　　　rickets n. 軟骨病　　　stunted adj. 發育不良的

contagious adj. 傳染性的　　　sun-drenched adj. 日照充足的　　　vaccination n. 接種疫苗

翻譯

　　生物感測器是一種植入身體內的微晶片，結合了無線溝通及全球定位科技來監控身體狀況和所在地理位置。例如，安妮的母親體內被植入一個小型的發送器微晶片，該發送器會持續傳送訊號到一座衛星，衛星會分析訊號並讓安妮知道她母親現在的確切位置。

　　生物感測器也能監控糖尿病患者身上的葡萄糖濃度。植入式晶片可在糖尿病患者的血糖過高或過低時警告患者，讓患者能趕快採取治療措施而不至於發病。一個內含微型探針的自黏式貼布會被貼在皮膚上，探針會使葡萄糖濃度得到最佳控制，並會朝貼布發出電子訊號，持續告知病患當下的葡萄糖濃度。

　　生物感測器在未來的醫學應用上有無限可能。會有越來越多的身體資訊獲得監控，協助病患和醫生雙方治療疾病及延長壽命。

　　生物感測器在非醫學領域的應用也在進行中。一種無線射頻辨識晶片已經進入測試階段。在身體植入微晶片的情況下，感應器能立即認出一個人，並允許該人進入保安區域內，例如軍事基地或高階政府情治單位。

　　雖然生物感測器必須先經過徹底測試才能獲得食品與藥物管理局的核准，有些人士認為，人類和機器人的之間的界線已快要被跨越。他們憂心生物感測器對人體來說可能會太具侵入性，該裝置也可能會傳遞太多資訊，使不肖份子或政府更容易控制和監控人民行為。也許可以發展出一套相關規定準則來消除他們的擔憂。

解析

1. 本篇第一段是生物感測器的簡介，後兩段詳述其使用方法，末段談及現況，故答案為(C)生物感測器的運用。(A)(B)(D)提及的只是各段的細節。

2. 第一、二、三段均談及生物感測器在醫療上的用途，第四段雖提到非醫療用途，卻並未提及確切的範疇，故選(D)。

3. 根據第二段 A self-adhesive patch...is placed on the skin，可知答案為(B)貼在皮膚上。

4. 見末段 Although biosensors have to be thoroughly tested before being approved by the FDA 可推斷仍未全面被測試過，故答案是(A)。

5. 由前面段落可知生物感測器須佩帶著，甚或植入體內，個人隱私資訊可能不保；因此可推斷它是(C)侵入性的。

biosensor n. 生物感測器　　transmitter n. 傳送器　　glucose n. 葡萄糖　　remedial adj. 治療的

patch n. 貼片　　probe n. 探針　　dispel vt. 消除 (煩惱，疑慮等)

翻譯

在天空和水之間閃耀的威尼斯是世界上最美麗的城市之一。它的暱稱是「*La Serenissima*」，意思是「最寧靜平和的」。然而，儘管作為一個受歡迎的浪漫景點，威尼斯卻越來越常成為險惡故事的背景都市。英國小說家大衛·修森就將威尼斯設為犯罪驚悚故事的場景，他表示，那是因為這個城市非常古老，並且「對死亡有一種非常天主教式的著迷。仔細看看那些教堂裡的繪畫，你會發現它們並非總是充滿喜樂。」

此外，城裡的建築本身也引發神秘幻想——魅影幢幢的宮殿，傾倒頹圮的別墅，遺棄廢置的造船廠，以及蜿蜒如迷宮的巷弄。除了偶爾出現的街燈或電視天線，威尼斯在過去四百年來並沒有太大改變。

正是在這座城市裡，在莎士比亞的《威尼斯商人》中，因猶太人受到的羞辱而憤怒不已的夏洛克堅持要求他該得的那一磅肉。愛與恨，正義與不公，貧民與貴族——這些是一直存在於威尼斯的矛盾。今日，上層階級，墮落的工匠、威尼斯的船夫、新來的觀光客和沿街兜售的移民小販，都是能寫成精彩故事的角色。威尼斯是作家能擷取或置放一個角色人物的好地方。

但現代的威尼斯非常缺乏空間。除非你非常有錢或是赫赫有名，你只能被埋在這裡著名的聖米迦勒墓園裡十年。「我在那裡的某一天有場掘骨儀式，」修森回憶道，「你可以從工人們拉起樸素的帆布，躲在陽光另一邊工作的舉動中看出來……有幾個問題躍入我腦海：萬一某個不是此人親戚的人早來一步，拿著偽造的文件要求開棺呢？又如果，當棺木被打開時，裡

面的東西卻出人意外？」他的話確實證明了，威尼斯也許看起來既美麗又平靜，卻也是個連死者都無法寧靜安息的地方。

解析

1. 根據第一段 Venice has become increasingly popular as the setting for more sinister stories，故選(C)。

2. 第一段提到：仔細看看那些教堂裡的繪畫，你會發現它們並非總是充滿喜樂。第二段提到威尼斯的建築物本身就有的神秘的氣氛。第三段指出威尼斯從上流社會到販夫走卒都能提供作家塑造書中人物的靈感，故知(A)羅曼蒂克和寧靜的氣氛不是威尼斯可以提供給修森的元素。

3. 由第四段得知威尼斯缺乏空間，除非是有錢人或重要人物，否則只能在公墓埋葬十年，故選(C)。

4. 第二段提到 Except for the occasional street lamp or TV antennae, Venice hasn't changed much over the past 400 years；可見前半句的兩樣東西不應出現在古代背景的電影中，故選(D)。

5. 由於關鍵字出現在第四段，前面談論缺乏墓地，到後面提到當「棺材打開」(coffin was opened)。可見是要把原來的屍體「挖掘出來」，讓位給後來者，故選(B)。

---

thriller n. 恐怖小說 (或電影)　　dockyard n. 造船廠　　labyrinthine adj. 錯綜複雜的；迷宮似的
antenna n. 天線　　impose vt. 把⋯強加於　　ghetto n. 貧民區　　patrician n. 貴族
artisan n. 工匠　　gondolier n. 搖平底船的船夫　　cemetery n. 公墓　　discreet adj. 樸素的

23 艾菲爾鐵塔：敢死士的夢想之塔
The Eiffel Tower: A Daredevil's Dream

翻譯

　　艾菲爾鐵塔這個著名地標驅使了刺激追求者在生命及健康受威脅下，甚至是構成犯罪的前提下表演大膽特技。

　　一長串多采多姿的歷史顯示，人們曾在這座塔上從事過各種稀奇古怪的舉動。1912 年，一個來自奧地利名叫法朗茲・瑞查的裁縫從第一層平台跳下幾近五十八公尺高，為的是測試他自己發明的降落傘外罩。不幸的是，他沒能活下來改善自己設計上的缺失。

　　1923 年，一名打賭輸了的法國記者皮耶・拉畢克從塔的一樓以騎腳踏車的方式往下一路騎完 347 階的樓梯。許多年後，他的同胞雨格・西查創下在十九分鐘內以腳踏車騎過 747 個階梯到達二樓的紀錄，一路上他的腳完全沒碰到地過。

　　1984 年，一對英國夫婦麥克・麥卡錫和亞曼達・塔克從最頂端的平台乘降落傘落下幾近兩百八十公尺之高。為了不讓他們專美於前，三年後，來自紐西蘭的海克特自二樓進行一百一十六公尺高的高空彈跳。同年，一個名叫羅伯特・莫拉提的美國人駕駛一架小型單引擎飛機從塔的拱形底部穿過。法國飛行員里昂・柯力特在 1926 年從事過同樣的冒險舉動，但在過程中因被陽光阻礙視線而撞毀。

　　1996 年的除夕夜，別名「蜘蛛人」的法籍敢死攀爬者亞朗・羅拔特，攀登上塔的西側，並精準地在剛好午夜時抵達頂端。後來他把這項舉動的困難度低調帶過，說：「畢竟，艾菲爾鐵塔不過就是個大梯子。」

　　有些冒險者為自己的瘋狂舉動付出致命代價。其他人，如拉畢克，則是在完成他們的特技表演後被警察逮捕並科以罰金。另外還有其他人較為幸運，在保證不再有下一次之後，得到一個嚴正警告了事。

　　也許這座塔太有名了，也許和它的獨特設計有關，也許只因為「它就在那裡」。無論原因是什麼，艾菲爾鐵塔似乎像一個巨大的磁鐵，吸引著驍勇之士或一勇之夫前來，並為此付出及高的代價。

解析

1. 首段 The Eiffel Tower has inspired thrill-seekers to risk life and limb,... 與末段 Whatever the reason, the Eiffel Tower seems to draw daredevils,...，顯示答案是(B)艾菲爾鐵塔吸引全世界的敢死隊來從事危險表演。(A)(C)(D)只是各段落的細節。

2. 根據第二段末句 Unfortunately, he never lived to improve on his flawed design 可知答案為(C)他為此而亡。

3. 第二段曾提及(B)降落傘；第三段有提及(A)騎腳踏車；(C)高空彈跳在第四段。只有溜輪式溜冰未曾提及，故選(D)。

4. 本題考文章細節。第四段 In 1984, ...three years later, ...and an American named Robert Moriarty flew a small, single-engine plane under the bottom arches 可知(A)敘述的年代錯誤，應該是 **1987** 年 (1984+3=1987)。

5. 第一段提及艾菲爾鐵塔吸引許多追求刺激的人 (thrill-seekers) 來表演一些大膽特技 (daring stunts)，由此可推論答案為(C)瘋狂的。

---

plunge vi. 落下，降下　　scale vt. 攀登　　downplay vt. 將…輕描淡寫　　feat n. 功績
zany adj. 瘋狂的　　stern adj. 嚴厲的　　foolhardy adj. 有勇無謀的

翻譯

　　狗擁有敏銳嗅覺這點是大家都知道的，據說比人類嗅覺靈敏數千倍。事實上，當狗出生時，牠們的眼睛是閉著的，約兩週之後才會張開，因此狗被迫仰賴嗅覺才能生存。

　　正是狗的這項出眾能力，使牠們被運用在重要的安檢工作上，例如作為尋找炸彈的偵測犬。狗只要在炸彈附近嗅聞一會兒，就能探查出炸彈所散發的些微化學氣味。

　　不久之前，科學家發明出會捕捉空氣樣本加以分析，藉此「聞出味道」的機器。炸彈偵測機器很快被介紹給世人，有些人預測，它們會取代狗的角色。機器有許多優點，像狗必須接受訓練，加以照顧，並不時需要休息，機器則可以被幾乎任何人持續不停地操作下去。炸彈偵測機如今被運用在許多機場，但它們並未取代偵測犬隊。

　　到目前為止，狗仍然最適合偵測大範圍地區如建築物或體育場。機器通常需要有一個可疑物體擺在前面才能適當發揮功能，然而狗卻可以四處巡視，自行尋找可疑物品。

　　真實的情況是，人類科技還不足以和狗與生俱來的能力相匹敵。事實上，人類仍在了解狗的嗅覺能力到底有多敏銳。就在最近幾年，科學家證明狗能只靠嗅聞人類的呼吸、皮膚或尿液就判別出癌細胞的存在。

　　因此，雖然科技每年都持續在進步，狗兒們似乎不太需要擔心。在未來一段時間，我們仍會需要這些無可取代的伙伴和牠們優異的能力。

解析

1. 由第三段 While dogs must be trained and cared for and have to rest every so often, the machines can be operated continuously by almost anyone 推知答案為(A)。

2. 根據第四段 Dogs are by far the best at examining large areas such as buildings or sports stadiums 推得答案(D)。

3. 根據第五段得知狗可以藉由嗅聞病人的呼吸、皮膚或尿液，偵測是否罹患癌症，故選(B)。

4. 第三段最後一句 but they (bomb-sniffing machines) have not replaced dog teams。第五段第二句 In fact, we are still learning just how powerful a dog's sense of smell can be。由此可做出結論，人類的科技和狗的潛能都有待開發，故選(C)。

5. 關鍵字原本是「相等物」的意思，而前一句提到狗靈敏的「嗅覺」，關鍵字前又提到人類，可見在句中是指前面狗有的東西並且人類也有的，可推得是人類的「嗅覺」，故選(C)。

---

snuffle vi. (動物) 嗅；聞　　displace vt. 取代；替代　　roam vt. 漫步　　irreplaceable adj. 無可替代的

翻譯

　　人為何會害怕蝙蝠？在世界上許多地方，蝙蝠被視為不祥之兆，因為牠們醜陋、怪異，又是夜行動物，亦即牠們活躍於夜間。即使在今日，一隻蝙蝠無聲飛過的黑暗身影仍能引發許多人的恐懼。再加上蝙蝠頭下腳上的詭異棲息習慣，更令許多人對這種動物倒胃口。

　　人們對蝙蝠有許多誤解。有些人堅持，蝙蝠會撞到人並傷害他們，因為他們認為蝙蝠的視力不好。另外有人相信，蝙蝠既骯髒又好戰。還有其他人覺得蝙蝠會纏在女性的頭髮裡並造成疾病。

　　人類傳統上對蝙蝠的恨意，也有許多科學化的理由，例如蝙蝠一直被報導會散播狂犬病。人們相信蝙蝠的飛行範圍廣大，因此會把致命的狂犬病毒傳染給更多動物。然而科學證實，只有極少數被傳染的蝙蝠能將狂犬病毒傳染給人，因為患病的蝙蝠很快就會死亡。科學家們也指出，每年死於蜂螫、猛犬攻擊或被雷殛的人類數量，都比被蝙蝠傳染到狂犬病的多許多。此外，一些關於蝙蝠會吸血的故事也不完全是虛構的。一種名為吸血蝙蝠的蝙蝠，確實會以溫血動物的血為食。牠們會用銳利的牙齒攻擊睡著的牛、狗、馬和鳥，再舔食傷口的血。但至於吸血蝙蝠會吸睡著的人類的血這種傳聞，則完全是謬誤，儘管牠們是有攻擊人類的能力。也許正是因為這種吸血習慣，使蝙蝠在無數的吸血鬼電影裡名垂千古。

　　事實上，蝙蝠是許多自然生態圈中重要的一環。各種在夜間開花的植物特別需要蝙蝠來授粉，若沒有蝙蝠，這些植物就會枯萎消失。蝙蝠也是優秀的天生掠食者，能控制害蟲和昆蟲的數目。牠們在許多方面對人類都有益，而我們對牠們抱持的一切誤解，對牠們實在很不公平。

解析

1. 本文共分四段；作者幾乎在每一段都指出人們對蝙蝠的誤解，結尾更強調這些誤解對蝙蝠不公平，故選(B)糾正人們對蝙蝠的誤解。
2. 由第三段中間部分知道吸血蝙蝠真的以動物的血為食，並描述其吸血方式，故知答案為(D)吸動物的血。
3. 見末段 Various night-blooming plants especially need bats for **pollination**，故選(C)幫助植物製造種子。
4. 因第三段 People believe that bats fly covering large areas and inflict the deadly rabies virus on more animals，故選(D)。
5. 從第一段的主題句 Why are people afraid of bats? 可推測本段重點在指出人們怕蝙蝠的事實。故從含有關鍵字的句子 The dark figure of a flying bat can incite fear in many people 可推測 incite 意指(A)引起。

nocturnal adj. 夜行的　　distaste n. 不喜歡　　militant adj. 好戰的　　rabies n. 狂犬病
inflict vt. 使⋯遭受　　rabid adj. 患狂犬病的　　lap vt. 舔　　pollination n. (植物) 授粉

翻譯

　　ScientificMatch.com 是一個由艾瑞克‧荷茲所創的新型線上交友網站。就像傳統的交友服務一樣，網站會員們必須提供照片和完整的個人資料，包括收入、家庭背景、宗教信仰、嗜好等等的一般資訊。不過，荷茲的公司比傳統交友配對方式還更先進一點：ScientificMatch.com 的會員們還必須提供一份 DNA 樣本。

　　荷茲的交友配對概念是以伯恩大學瑞士籍研究員克勞司‧維迪根博士所提出的「汗濕 T 恤研究」為基礎。維迪根的假設是，如同動物會在跟對方建立親密關係之前先嗅聞彼此的味道一樣，人類也會對其他人類所散發的味道產生反應。接著他進行一項研究，要求女性嗅聞不同男性穿了三天的 T 恤，而且必須說出哪件 T 恤的味道聞起來最好。得到結果之後，維迪根分析了參與這項實驗的男性與女性的 DNA，並特別專注在一組被稱為 MHC (主要組織相容複體) 的基因上。這些基因是構成免疫系統的一部份，免疫系統協助身體擊退疾病，並決定經由手術進行的移植最後是否能被身體接受。

　　不過，這些基因也同樣影響人類所分泌出的汗液味道，使每個人有屬於自己的獨特體味。維迪根發現，具有某一組 MHC 基因的女性，會偏好擁有另一組非常不同 MHC 基因的男性所穿的 T 恤，反之亦然。從演化的觀點來看，這是有道理的，因為由擁有相當不同種類基因的父母所生下的孩子，免疫力會比較強，也較能抵抗疾病。這聽起來很不浪漫，但根據人們的 DNA 來替他們配對，也許有助於幫他們找到彼此的靈魂伴侶。

解析

1. 本文主要在解釋如何將「汗溼 T 恤研究」此理論應用在為人們介紹適合的異性，故選(A)。
2. 根據文章最後一句 but matching people according to their DNA might help **find their soul mates** 可知答案為(D)找到適合的伴侶。
3. 由第三段知道具有某一類 MHC 基因的女性比較喜歡具有「不同類」MHC 基因的男性所穿的 T 恤，反之亦然，故選(D)。
4. 由第三段得知父母親基因類型變化較大，所生的小孩免疫力較強，比較不容易生病，故選(A)。
5. 因為第二段提到動物建立關係前，先嗅聞彼此的氣味，所以 exude 應指(B)「散發出」氣味。

---

histocompatability n. 組織相容性　　　transplant n. 移植手術　　　vice versa adv. 反之亦然

翻譯

　　近來有許多關於全球暖化的討論，但另一個引起關切的問題則是全球黯化。科學家們發出警告，地球不只逐漸暖化，也在逐漸變暗中。當空氣污染導致照射到地球表面的光照量降低時，就產生了全球黯化現象。乍聽之下，這似乎是件好事，因為這麼一來似乎就能降低全球溫度升高的危機。然而，這個有利有弊的現象實際上掩蓋了全球暖化的真相。

　　全球黯化和全球暖化都是由燃燒石化燃料如石油或瓦斯所產生的煙塵而導致。在全球黯化的情況中，石化燃料的使用污染了空氣，而污染物黏附在雲上，使它們把更多放射線反彈回太空，結果導致照射到地表上的陽光減少。此外，這也使陽光和熱無法到達地球，使地球變得比以往寒冷。

　　有些人認為，全球黯化使科學家對全球暖化的真正危機掉以輕心。「它 (全球黯化) 是個令人不安的現象。」英國科學家傑拉得・史坦希爾如此表示。他是最初發覺到這種如雙面刃般的驚人現象，並為其命名的人。根據研究指出，若沒有全球黯化現象，全球暖化現象原本應該會造成全球溫度上升攝氏 6 度，而不是只有 0.6 度。雖然表面上看來，全球黯化抵銷了全球暖化問題，但實際上並沒有。更糟的是，這使得科學家沒有去尋找因應之道，以正確解決我們現在或將來所面臨的問題。

　　結果科學家如今建議，全球應該同時一起處理這兩項問題，方式是減少使用石化燃料。全球黯化問題被揭露後，它應該成為一項轉變的契機，使人們不再埋首沙中對問題視而不見，而是埋首於解決問題。

解析

1. 由第二段可知全球暖化與全球黯化都起因於過度燃燒石化燃料所引起的空氣污染。第三段可知雖然全球黯化降低了地球的溫度，卻並未解決全球暖化的問題。最後一段第一句：科學家建議大家減少使用石化燃料才能同時解決全球暖化與全球黯化，故選(C)。

2. 由第二段 It prevents sunlight and heat from reaching the earth and makes the earth **cooler** than before 得知答案為(A)幫助降低地球溫度。

3. 由第三段的...English scientist Gerald Stanhill, who first spotted the...and **coined** the term 可知答案為(D)傑拉得・史坦希爾創造了「全球黯化」這個詞。

4. doubled-edged sword 指的是雙面皆可傷人的劍；由第三段中間部分可推論這個字在此指的是空氣污染所造成的全球暖化與全球黯化問題，故選(C)。

5. 見第二段，作者解釋全球黯化形成的原因，空氣污染導致雲層變厚，陽光較不能照到地球，亦即陽光減弱，故選(B)減少。

---

a mixed blessing　n.　有利有弊的事情　　　soot　n.　煙塵　　　spot　vt.　發覺，發現　　　offset　vt.　抵銷

翻譯

　　人類燃燒石化燃料，製造出大量二氧化碳。幸運的是，其中約三分之一都被海洋吸收，減緩了全球暖化所造成的影響。然而，這種平衡作用卻也可能迫使一些海洋動物瀕臨絕種。

　　自然狀態下的海洋呈鹼性而非酸性，這有助一些無脊椎生物如珊瑚和蛤蜊等利用鈣來形成外殼和骨骼。然而，當二氧化碳和海水混合時，會形成導致鈣被溶解的碳酸。

　　2008年二月，哈佛大學的安德魯·科納爾指出，化石紀錄中已經顯示海水酸化的危險。約兩億五千萬年前，地球經歷到史上最大的一場生物滅絕災難。可能的原因有：火山以無比龐大的規模爆發，使空氣中充滿令生物窒息的二氧化碳，造成百分之九十的海綿和珊瑚類生物滅絕。如果全球暖化現象持續下去，到了2100年，珊瑚類生物會面臨到同樣情況，無法在南方海洋中存活。

　　其他海洋無脊椎生物也會大難臨頭。加州大學的葛瑞琴·郝夫曼一直在研究紫海膽，那是一種生活在潮間帶岩石間的小型有刺生物。郝夫曼創造出一個假設排碳量並未改善，預估一百年後將會變成的環境，並在其中培育紫海膽。結果，海水中增加的酸度加上變熱的水溫將造成致命影響，海膽必須比平常努力三倍才能製造出骨骼，而且即使製造出來了，骨骼也是畸形的。

　　對珊瑚和海膽等海洋生物可能造成的毀滅，不只會影響到牠們自身的生存。特別拿珊瑚來說，沒有了珊瑚，會使許多生物失去棲息地和食物來源，造成的影響將是毀滅性的。

　　鑑於以上這些殘酷的可能性，期望海洋能減緩地球暖化效應的人，也許需要三思了。

解析

1. 根據第一段 Nevertheless, the same balanced act may also force some marine animals to the edge of extinction，故選(D)指出全球暖化對海洋生物的傷害。
2. 第二段指出海水本是鹼性的，其中的鈣質有助於形成珊瑚的骨骼或蛤蠣的殼。但是二氧化碳溶解於海水，使其形成酸性，溶解鈣質，對上述生物造成傷害，故選(C)。
3. 由第一段的 **Fortunately**「幸好」，可以推測答案為(B)海洋可以減緩全球暖化效應。
4. 第五段提到珊瑚的死亡將消滅許多物種的棲息地和食物，故選(D)很多其他海洋生物依靠珊瑚提供棲息地和食物。此外，第三段提及的大爆炸所提供的內容無法斷定是否「對海膽沒有影響」，故(A)非正解。(C)應修正為「在較熱、且為酸性的環境中，海膽會畸形。」
5. 由第五段上下文判斷，關鍵字應為負面語意，故選(A)災難性的。

---

alkaline adj. 鹼性的　　acidic adj. 酸性的　　spineless adj. 無脊椎的　　invertebrate n. 無脊椎動物　　clam n. 蛤蜊　　carbolic acid 碳酸　　sea urchin n. 海膽　　spiny adj. 多刺的　　deformed adj. 畸形的　　grim adj. 無情的

29 小狗如廁訓練記
Puppy Poop Preparation

翻譯

　　對麥克斯而言，那真是個漫長的下午。吃過午餐後不久，平常的例行活動就被兩名陌生人給打斷。他們帶他坐了好久的車，抵達一棟陌生的房子。他一到那裡，就花了一分鐘左右在客廳繞著圈踱步。就在那時，他做了一件錯事。麥克斯注意到那兩名陌生人立刻朝他奔過來，其中一個人將他抱到一旁，另一個人則蹲下來檢視地毯上一塊嶄新的潮濕污漬。這兩名陌生人對他的舉動似乎不太高興。

　　那兩名陌生人其中之一就是我，而我跟新養的小狗麥克斯相處的第一個下午可不太順利。把這隻可愛的八週大小狗抱進屋裡幾分鐘後，我和我妻子就明白到，為了麥克斯和我們的地毯好，我們得好好學習一下如何訓練小狗上廁所！

　　我們發現，小狗新到一個地方時，會建立起一塊用來睡覺的地方，一般稱為他們的窩，而所有窩以外的地方都可以用來上廁所。

　　上廁所訓練在隔天開始。我妻子和我在麥克斯吃完飯後就小心地盯著他。通常小狗會在吃完飯後約三十至四十五分鐘上廁所，想當然爾，麥克斯就在吃完早餐後半小時開始嗅聞客廳地面。我趕快抱起麥克斯，把他帶到花園一角，讓他在那裡上廁所。我稱讚麥克斯做得好，並給他一小片狗餅乾作為獎賞。

　　然而，那天早上我只是運氣好。那天稍晚，我沒有那麼仔細注意麥克斯的行為，他開始繞圈走路，而我還來不及跑過去抓起他，他就已經在一塊地毯上留下一小坨便便了。我很失望，但我並沒有因為他犯錯而懲罰他，因為他很可能不知道自己哪裡做錯了，這樣只會拖慢如廁訓練的過程。

　　到那週結束時，麥克斯已經大有進步。這隻溫順的狗兒逐漸把整個房子當作他的窩，只在花園裡解放。

解析

1. 本文從作者第一天抱養小狗說起，第二段開始談到小狗的便便訓練，接下來的各段述說訓練過程，故選⒟小狗的如廁訓練過程。
2. 由末段 By the end of the week, Max was making good progress 得知答案為⒝。
3. 根據第三段 And all new putties treat any place away from their den a suitable place to go to the toilet，故選⒞。
4. 因末段 The docile dog gradually treated the whole house as an extension of his den 故知麥克斯現在是⒝一隻服從的成犬。
5. 因第四段 I quickly picked Max up and carried him over to a corner of the garden 得知小狗被訓練在花園上廁所，而末段..., only did his business in the garden 可推測小狗是在花園⒜上廁所。

bound vi. (高興大步地) 跑　　den n. (動物的) 窩，巢　　docile adj. 溫馴的

挑戰極限

翻譯

對許多人而言，老式的旅行已變得乏善可陳而不夠刺激。他們不想再住奢華飯店、在遺跡間漫步、在熱門景點前照相留念或購買紀念品了。相反地，他們想做另一種不同的探索。體驗各種文化和環境當然不錯，但他們的興趣更在於探索自身。因此，他們想要的假期就被稱為「冒險假期」和「極限假期」。

冒險假期自然是活動滿檔，通常會有需要體力的活動如登山健行、徒步或騎單車跋山涉水。這些行程的重點並不在於讓你感到放鬆或受到文化洗禮，反而較在於藉由貼近大自然和實際體驗其他生活方式，讓你感覺到生命的奔騰。例如，你可以選擇踩著單車騎完整條萬里長城的行程。若騎單車對你來說輕而易舉，你也可以選擇難度高的登山健行活動。有些套裝行程讓參加者能攀登有「非洲屋脊」之稱的吉力馬札羅山。你甚至能乘坐長途巴士跨越沙漠或絲路。在這些假期中，你的暫時棲身之處是什麼？通常會是荒野中的一頂帳棚。因為冒險假期往往就是登山健行、騎單車、乘坐地方大眾運輸工具和露營。旅行者不只在身體上受到考驗，也藉此更加貼近活生生存在於他們周圍的各種文化。

另一方面，極限假期則更加地……嗯……極端。在這類假期中，參加者的目的不在於和異國環境或人民相遇，而在於找尋能在身體上、心理上和精神上有挑戰的地方和情境。他們會找尋能盡可能潛入最深處的水域、能從一台飛機上跳出去進行高空跳傘的晴朗天空，還有能在上面作高空彈跳的高聳橋樑。他們會以閃電般的速度乘雪滑板滑下火山，在極度洶湧湍急的洪流中泛舟。他們喜好從事極限運動，因為這讓他們能瞭解自己體能和理智的極限何在。簡而言之，他們從事這些挑戰死神般的特技，讓自己能特別體會到正在活著以及能夠生存下來的感覺。

解析

1. 本篇文章主要是談論兩種新型的渡假方式，所以最可能刊登在休閒雜誌上，故選(B)。
2. 第二段提到冒險假期的重點不是要讓人放輕鬆，而是要讓人接近自然、體驗不同的生活方式。第三段所描述的極限假期都是在大自然的環境中挑戰人的身心極限。由此可見(A)讓渡假客接近自然為其共同特色。至於(C)渡假者要花費大筆金錢，(D)有機會品嚐當地美食，文章皆未提及。
3. 第二段最後一句，對等連接詞 but 所連接的對等子句，主詞應都是 tourists，因此 them 是指(B)。
4. 由第三段 They are into extreme sports so they can realize the limitations of their bodies and courage，也就是所謂的「自我探索、自我發現」，故選(D)。
5. 由第二段指出冒險假期的重點不是要讓人放輕鬆，故可推論(C)此種渡假方式不太可能吸引想休閒 (leisurely) 渡假的人士為答案。此外，由第二段描述冒險假期的內容看來，也很需要體力和嘗試的勇氣，且文章沒有線索提到何者需要較多體力和勇氣，故(D)非正解。

---

stale　adj.　無新意的　　　trek　vi.　艱苦地跋涉　　　cakewalk　n.　輕而易舉的事情　　　torrent　n.　洪流，急流

翻譯

　　人類本質上具有跟彼此溝通的需求，即使是世界各地的聽障人士都發展出一套使用手勢和姿勢進行交談的方法。手語就跟任何口說語言一樣，會因國家而異。由於一些人士的熱心努力，供聽障人士使用的標準手語逐漸發展出來。

　　西元 1620 年，第一本教授手語的書籍在義大利出版。超過 130 年後，巴黎的亞貝·查爾斯·米謝·德雷斐為聽障人士創立第一所免費學校。在這所學校中，他結合一些已經由聽障者建立起的溝通手勢及自創手勢，形成法文版的手語。他的努力為日後標準手語的建立鋪了路。

　　在美國，湯馬斯·霍普金斯·戈勞德為了幫助一名鄰居的女兒，在 1815 年赴法國學習手語。他帶回一名聽障教師，並於 1817 年在美國建立第一所聽障學校。在戈勞德的影響之下，美式手語 (ASL) 和法式手語 (FSL) 變得相當近似。1864 年，戈勞德的兒子愛德華成為美國第一所也是唯一的聽障人士人文大學首位校長，該校也以他為名，叫做戈勞德大學。這所大學變成國際聽障人士間最重要的教育中心之一。

　　在中國，第一所聽障學校是在 1887 年由一位名叫米爾斯的美國傳教士創立。然而，美式手語並未對中式手語 (CSL) 有太大影響，原因在於書寫語言的不同。以英語書寫的語言是拼音文字——亦即每個字母都代表一個音。因為許多聽障人士無法區分聲音，於是他們的手語就從動作或概念發展而來。但中式書寫語言是象形文字，因此手語就會由已經形成的文字形象為基礎而發展。

　　即便有語言上的種種不同，聽障人士仍和彼此緊密結合，形成一套以手語為中心的豐富多樣文化。

解析

1. 根據第一段 Sign language **varies between countries** just as any spoken language 得知答案為(A)。

2. 由第四段最後一句 On the other hand, the Chinese written language is **pictorial**, so the signs follow the already established pictures 得知答案為(C)。

3. 根據第二段 His efforts (指法國人亞貝的努力) paved the way for a standard form of sign language，故選(B)。

4. 由第二段得知亞貝創立的是在法國給聽障人士的第一所免費學校，而第三段指出聾人可以上的第一所大學是設立於美國的戈勞德大學，故選(D)。

5. 見第一段 Humans have an intrinsic need to communicate. Even the deaf throughout the world have developed a way to talk using signs and gestures 可知人類有天生的需要去與人溝通；即便是聾人，也會發展出手語來與人交談，故選(C)天生的。

---

hearing-impaired adj. 有聽力障礙的　　namesake n. 同名的人 / 事 / 物　　phonetic adj. 拼音的
pictorial adj. 圖畫的

　　根據最近一項由哈佛大學所進行的研究指出，消費者越來越重視道德議題。一項貼有合理勞動環境保證標籤的商品，即使標價較高，都還是比沒有此標籤的同類商品更易售出。難怪，如今許多企業比以往更認真看待自身所負有的企業社會責任 (CSR)，以求增添產品的吸引力。

　　其他統計數字顯示，四分之三的英國消費者有興趣購買具有符合勞動標準及「綠色」環保憑證的產品。被標明符合這些標準的商品往往大為熱賣。但買下這類產品的消費者是否真的做了正確選擇？不幸的是，並非所有訴諸倫理議題的銷售策略都誠實地恪遵自身所宣稱的標準。許多公司在對自身產品所披掛的「倫理」或「綠色」徽章做出漂亮宣稱的同時，會掩蓋事實或甚至撒些小謊。

　　無論在企業界或消費者之間，注重環保都是正在全球增長的趨勢。大多數消費者都樂於為改善環境盡一點力。然而，並沒有太多消費者願意為此大費周章。他們只想要品質好又不會比其他替代選擇貴太多的產品。另一方面，若他們能很方便地取得價格低廉、包裝精美而品質尚可的「非綠色」不環保商品，他們也會樂於轉而選擇它們。

　　面對這種情況，銷售「綠色」商品的企業就得學會如何找到平衡點。積極促銷商品「不會破壞環境」的「綠色」特點，並不一定保證成功。企業必須說服消費者，購買此產品將使他們在個人和環境層次都能獲益。消費者個人的獲益考量可能包括健康、節能和划算等。「價格低廉」對大多數消費者而言仍然是主要購買

誘因。威名百貨曾在某一則廣告中宣稱：「若環保商品不能拯救人們的荷包，是無法拯救地球的。」這句話似乎相當確切地表明了它的立場。

1. 文章顯示消費者愈來愈有環保觀念，有意願購買「綠色產品」；而企業也看準這個趨勢，推出「綠色產品」，故選(D)。(C)質疑「道德」銷售的可信度指的是第二段最後提到某些公司隱瞞產品事實，這是細節，而非文章主旨。
2. 第一段最後一句提到企業比以往注重企業社會責任，為的是增加產品的吸引力，亦即(C)在市場上得到競爭優勢。
3. 第三段指出消費者希望「綠色」產品品質佳，又不會比較貴。但是如果「非綠色」產品品質優、包裝吸引人，而且比較便宜，消費者就會選擇購買後者。此外，第四段第五句 "Lower prices" still remains the major allure for most customers 最為關鍵，故選(A)。
4. 第四段前面提到販賣「綠色」產品的公司要取得平衡；一味的用激進手法促銷不見得能獲利。這意味著如果設定合理價格，讓消費者買得起，買賣雙方就都能對環保有所貢獻，故選(C)。至於(A)綠色標記的產品「無可避免地」比較昂貴，文章並無這麼武斷的顯示。
5. hit the nail on its head 這個片語字面上是「敲釘子敲在釘頭上」，亦即「說得或做得恰到好處 (抓到重點)；一針見血；正中要害」。放在文章裡是指威名的廣告詞說的有道理：「環保產品如果不能替人省 (save) 錢，也就不能拯救 (save) 地球。」故選(B)。

credential n. 證書　　abide vi. 遵守　　conscientious adj. 憑良心的；誠實的　　grandiose adj. 誇張的
procure vt. 取得，獲得　　decent adj. 像樣的

我們的 X 檔案：誇張怪異一籮筐
Our X-files: Xaggerated and Xtraordinary

翻譯

　　數十年來，不明飛行物體 (簡稱 UFO) 一直引起熱烈辯論。世界各地目睹不明飛行物的報告頻傳。一名美國人喬治・費勒對近來美國和世界各地的不明飛行物目睹事件作出整理。一具不明飛行物被形容為一個會飛的黑色三角形物體，正中間有一道光往下照射；另一具則是會改變顏色的圓盤形物體。有時候一個發出神秘閃光的物體可能是一架小型飛機，也可能是過度想像力作祟。

　　1938 年 10 月 30 日，一齣名為《世界大戰》的廣播劇意外在紐約和紐澤西引起大眾恐慌。即使報紙在對該劇的介紹中聲明它是虛構作品，仍有數千名民眾相信紐澤西正遭受火星人的轟炸攻擊。他們打電話到警局，要求警方協助他們躲避毒氣突襲並從市區疏散。

　　該齣廣播劇開頭是一場平常的歌舞節目秀，接著突然插播一則新聞快報，以跟真實新聞快報一樣的方式報導火星人正侵略地球的消息。有些聽眾因驚嚇和過度激動被送進醫院治療。據報一名婦女瀕臨自殺邊緣，因為她寧願死在自己手中而不是火星人手裡。警方和其他官方單位極力說服民眾，告訴大家這只是個廣播節目，並沒有外星人入侵地球。

　　另外一項已出現超過一百年，但至今仍無法解釋的情況是馬爾法的鬼光。有數千名民眾晚間在德州西部窺視著奇昂地山，找尋神秘鬼光的蹤影。這些光沒有明顯來源，沒有確切的出現地點，但它們會移動和發光。有些人說它們是持續發亮的白色光，有些人說它們是會移動的彩色光。有些人看到三種光芒，又有人看到多達十種。曾有人試圖研究這些光，但每當

人們接近時，光就消失了。

　　今日，有《X 檔案》等電視影集及各種聲稱是外星人真實見證的特別節目，不明飛行物的故事也將繼續下去。

解析

1. 第一段描述人們對不明飛行物體有不同的敘述，第二、第三段則提到對於收音機所播放有關不明飛行物體的廣播劇竟信以為真，可見人們頗在意不明飛行物體的存在，故選(B)。
2. 由第二段、第三段得知《世界大戰》其實是廣播劇，故選(C)。
3. 見第一段 One UFO was described as a flying black triangle with **light** in the middle beaming down 以及 Sometimes an object with mysterious **lights** 可以判定不明飛行物體大多會發光，故選(D)。
4. 由第四段得知人們試著研究馬爾法的鬼光，但一接近光就消失了，所以尚未被證明其到底所為何物，故(A)為非。
5. 由關鍵片語後面的 **suicide** 一字，以及 **claiming** 後的敘述可推測答案為(B)。

---

beam　vi. 照射　　overactive　adj. 過於活躍的　　raid　n. 襲擊，侵襲　　news flash　n. 新聞快報
frenzy　n. 極度的激動

34 銷售與味道
Selling and Smelling

　　背景音樂、視覺擺設和商品樣本一同使商店變成一座心怡神悅的天堂。有些生意人也相信，味道的運用亦有助提升銷售成績。

　　這個概念被稱作「氣味行銷」，目標在於透過消費者的嗅覺來吸引他們。店家會用人工香氣來營造出某種心情，甚至強化店裡所售產品的味道。這些味道可能經由一個簡單的噴灑系統散播，但還有一種鞋盒大小的隱藏機器讓店家能變換味道。

　　有些研究支持這種行銷手法。《品牌感受》一書的作者馬丁・林斯東指出，對百分之八十的男性及百分之九十的女性而言，味道會使他們想起深刻而感性的回憶。這是因為嗅覺記憶被貯存在大腦的「邊緣系統」，那裡也是掌管情緒的神經中樞。因此，若那些味道連結到一段正面的記憶或情緒，就有可能鼓勵消費者購買某項產品，或至少在店內停留。

　　也許是因為巧克力的香甜味會連結到兒時記憶，這種味道相當受店家歡迎。例如 2006 年時，就有一個美國手機商店將高濃度的巧克力味道散播在店內展示的一系列巧克力色的手機四周，企圖營造出一種愉快的購物氛圍。

　　然而，香味不是對每個人都有成功的吸引作用。對香味的反應是非常個人的，因此某位消費者聞起來覺得很香的味道，卻可能引發另一名消費者的反感。有些店經理也擔心此舉會污染空氣，甚至使某些患病的顧客產生呼吸問題。但隨著充斥各處的符號、顏色及音樂，有些店家勢必會繼續嘗試這種行銷手法——只要能與眾不同。

解析

1. 第一段最後一句 Some businesspeople also believe that the use of the smells could help build up sales，而其後各段則提出理論基礎及實際作法，故選(C)。
2. 第三段指出有些研究支持這種促銷方式，故選(B)。不過第二段最後一句指出鞋盒大小的隱藏機器讓店家能變換味道，可見顧客無從得知，所以(D)不對。
3. 因第四段提到實際運用巧克力味道以製造宜人的購物氣氛來銷售巧克力手機的例子，故知(C)散播巧克力的宜人香氣為答案。
4. 第五段一開始指出對某種氣味的反應，因人而異。所以(A)此法僅對女性顧客管用是錯誤的。
5. 因關鍵字前一句的 sense of smell 而知答案為(D)。文章各處出現的 smell 近義字尚有 scent、aroma、odor。

reinforce vt. 加強；強化　　olfactory adj. 嗅覺的　　limbic n. 邊緣系統　　neurological adj. 神經的
diffuse vi./vt. 使(氣體、熱、光等)擴散

翻譯

　　自乾燥不毛的沙漠巍然升起 350 公尺，佔地約 9.4 公里的艾爾斯岩位於澳洲北領地，是世界上最大的單塊岩石，或稱獨塊巨石。這座壯觀岩石由多種不同的礦物構成，因此顏色會因白天陽光入射角度改變而神奇地變換。它是在西元 1873 年被一名歐洲探險者發現，並以南澳總督亨利・艾爾斯爵士的名字為它命名。此後一百年間，這座岩石變成熱門觀光景點。觀光客們興致勃勃地踩著岩石上的小路，抵達最頂端。很少人注意到居住在這座岩石附近那些身軀半裸的「未開化」原住民。

　　早期的觀光客對此地原住民和那座岩石間的深刻關係一無所知，直到 1960 年代，人類學家對這些被忽略的居民進行研究才真相大白。原住民將這座岩石稱為「烏魯魯」，在他們的神話中佔有中心位置。這座獨塊巨石是他們最神聖的場所，是世界上一切能量的中心，許多祖輩的和近似神的存在者住在那裡，活在「夢時間」中，亦即地球創造的時刻。原住民在岩石中保存著許多洞窟壁畫，描述來自夢時間的神話。獨塊巨石上的大小石頭都有特別的象徵意義，例如有的是超自然生物的部分實體或武器，當創造時刻結束時，它們就以那種樣貌被凍結在永恆中。

　　澳洲政府在瞭解到這個地點對原住民的重要性後，他們使這些原住民在 1985 年成為這座岩石的法定擁有者。如今原住民們將此地整頓成一座國家公園，靠觀光收入和政府補助來維持運作。原住民不會攀爬到獨塊巨石的頂峰，他們也希望觀光客們不要這麼做。雖然許多觀光客無視他們的冀望仍選擇攀登上去，還是有越來越多人以更虔誠的態度對待這個地點，只是到那裡欣賞這個神秘的地方，一同分享這座神奇岩石的傳統守護者們擁有的神話和文化。

解析

1. 本文第一段談及澳洲國家公園中的艾爾斯巨石的特質及其被發現的歷史。而第二段、第三段講到，人們起初不解這塊巨石對當地原住民的重要性及其神聖性，漸漸地，經由人類學家與當地原住民的努力人們總算理解，故選(C)。

2. 見第二段 The monolith is their most sacred site. It is the very center of the world's energy, ...故選(D)。

3. 見第三段 The Aborigines themselves now manage it as a **national park**，故選(B)。

4. 由第一段可知此巨石是歐洲探險家發現的，他只是以當時的南澳總督亨利・艾爾斯爵士的名字來命名巨石，而不是艾爾斯爵士發現此巨石，故(A)為非。

5. 由關鍵字前的敘述知道此巨石對當地原住民有其神聖的意義，原住民絕不會大不敬地爬上巨石，他們也不希望觀光客這麼做 (見末段 Although many tourists ignore their wishes and opt to make the climb, more and more people are treating the site more reverently) 。由此可推測答案是(A)尊敬地。

---

monolith　n.　獨塊巨石　　　　arid　adj.　乾旱的，不毛的　　　angles of incidence　n.　入射角
alternative　adj.　替代的　　　tramp　vi.　踩；腳步沈重地走　　　boulder　n.　卵石

翻譯

　　在商場內播放自家電視廣告的作法，在全球許多大型零售量販店內如雨後春筍般出現。商家可藉由直接在店內播放廣告的方式，提醒消費者之前曾經看過的廣告、介紹新商品、促銷特價品以及告知更多店內商品訊息。再者，約有四分之三的購買決定是在店內做的，這也使登廣告變得越來越吸引人。

　　世界上最大的零售量販店威名百貨，就是以這種方式在全美超過三千家店內透過電視螢幕讓顧客看見。約有 140 個生產商砸錢在這些螢幕上登廣告，而資料顯示，銷售量也因為這項促銷策略提昇了百分之二。百分之二的銷售量成長也許聽起來不是很多，但別忘了，威名百貨在 2007 年的獲利超過 11 兆美金。英國的特易購也以同樣方式獲益——有些特定目標品牌的銷售量竟增加了百分之二十五！

　　在一些新興市場國裡，許多商家也採用這種會賺錢的廣告方式。全球第二大的量販商家樂福，就已在位於波蘭的店內設置電視，並開始在巴西如法炮製。在中國大陸，一個名為焦點媒體的廣告商正協助商家裝設這項服務。

　　在過去幾年試行店內電視廣告行銷的經驗中，企業主對這項行銷手法也多了些瞭解。例如，消費者不太可能站著不動看完一則三十秒的傳統廣告，五到十五秒的小廣告才最有效。此外，無止境地播送廣告往往會使潛在買家卻步。為了克服這點，店家會在廣告間插入各式主題的小片段，如天氣、娛樂和烹飪。

　　店內電視廣告行銷在二十一世紀初才開始受到歡迎。即使有一些統計數據攤在眼前，還是沒有人能確定它的效果到底有多好。目前的實際情況是：以這種方式作廣告的公司，有百分之八十都能續約。因此，店內電視廣告行銷有可能就此常駐店內了。

解析

1. 由文章的頭、尾兩段可以看出主旨在討論「商店內設置電視打廣告」的行銷手法，故選(C)。
2. (A)提供購物者最近的新聞顯然和購物、促銷的功能毫無關連。
3. 波蘭出現在第三段，因為這個國家擁有新興的市場潛力，世界第二大的零售商家樂福已開始在其商店內使用本文介紹的廣告手法，故選(B)。
4. mushroom 原為「蘑菇」，是一種生長非常迅速的蕈類植物。在第一段當動詞，根據大意，可以猜測是用於比喻迅速發展，如雨後春筍般出現，故選(B)。
5. 最後一段提到百分之八十使用此種廣告手法的公司都續簽了合約。由此推測答案為(D)這些公司都蒙受其利。

appealing adj. 有魅力的　　lucrative adj. 獲利的　　kit out 裝設　　miscellaneous adj. 各式各樣的
bit n. 片段

37 促成凝塊的一針
A Shot for Clot

　　血友病是一種出血疾病。正常情況下，若我們受傷並開始流血，血液中的蛋白質會幫助血液凝固。血友病患身上缺乏這些蛋白質，因此可能會因為刮傷或割傷而流血至死。然而，對這些患者來說，真正的問題在於流入肌肉和關節中的內出血。在一些嚴重的案例中，內出血可能會在無任何明顯原因的情況下自然地發生。

　　血友病是一種遺傳疾病，患者體內缺少負責凝固血液的基因或基因無法發揮正常功能。這些基因存在於 X 染色體中，有血友病的男性會將這種基因傳給女兒，因為女性會從父親身上遺傳到 X 染色體。但因為女生有兩個 X 基因，所以女兒不會得血友病。而男性血友病患者的兒子也不會得血友病，因為他們會遺傳到父親身上正常的 Y 染色體。若一名女性身上帶有血友病基因，她將此病遺傳給子女的機率是百分之五十。

　　血友病也有「皇室病」之稱，因為它在十九世紀時影響到數名歐洲皇室成員。維多利亞女王的第八個兒子就得了血友病，在三十一歲時死亡。女王還有兩名女兒身上帶有血友病基因，其中一名女兒將此基因遺傳給 1904 年出生的亞烈克斯太子，亦即俄國沙皇尼古拉二世之子。有傳聞表示，血友病在這整個家族的衰敗過程中推了最後一把。

　　拜現代醫療科學之賜，醫師們已經開發出能取代遺失的凝血因子的藥。當身體內部開始出血時就必須注入足夠的因子才能形成血液凝塊。替代因子的發展，使血友病患者也有可能活得健康或更久。

解析

1. 本文主要談論血友病，第二段是起因，末段是治療方法，故選(D)。(A)(B)(C)僅是各段的細節。

2. 由第二段開頭 Hemophilia is genetic 的 genetic 得知此病與基因有關，故選(C)遺傳的。

3. 由第二段 But none of the daughters will have hemophilia since they have two X genes 得知女兒不會得血友病，故選(B)。

4. 見第四段 : thanks to modern medical science, doctors have created drugs that replace the missing clotting factor，故選(A)。第三段提到血友病雖曾影響歐洲皇家成員，以 only 來敘述卻武斷不實，故不選(B)。由第二段得知血友病的基因存在於 X 染色體，故(C)應改為 It's the father who carries the hemophilia genes to his daughter。由第三段得知血友病害俄羅斯沙皇的家族衰敗，而非維多利亞的家族，故不選(D)。

5. 見第一段 Normally, if we get hurt and start to bleed, the proteins in our blood cause it to clot 可判斷 clot 指「凝結」，故選(B)。

hemophilia n. 血友病　　protein n. 蛋白質　　deficient adj. 不足的，缺乏的
genetic adj. 基因的，遺傳的　　dysfunctional adj. 不正常的　　chromosome n. 染色體
downfall n. 沒落

翻譯

　　生活中總是會有生日、節日或其他特殊場合需要送人禮物。然而，隨著世界變得越來越多樣化，要找到最適合的禮物也變成一件越來越複雜的事。有時候雖然你是出於好意送禮，對來自另一個文化的人而言，禮物本身所傳達出的意義卻可能就沒那麼好了。

　　送禮在日本和韓國等國家的文化裡是必不可少的。在接受禮物之前先推拒一番被認為是非常有禮貌的表現。此外用雙手送禮或收禮表示出你的尊敬。在韓國，贈送尖銳物品象徵著你要跟對方絕交，送手帕則代表哀悼。在日本，送數目是四或九的禮物會被認為是不吉利的。

　　中東國家則有自己獨特的送禮習俗。此地區大多數國家有類似禮節，因為這些禮節跟人們的宗教信仰有關。在伊斯蘭教中，絕對只能用右手送禮跟收禮，這點很重要。穿戴金或絲綢來顯示自己的財富是有違伊斯蘭教信仰的，所以，最好把這些物品從你的禮物清單上剔除。還有，狗的圖片被認為不潔，也可能讓送禮活動蒙上陰影。幸運的是，你只需要送禮物給生活中跟你很親密的人，而最適合的禮物就是指南針，因為它會指出伊斯蘭教的聖地——麥加的方向。

　　來自拉丁美洲的人較儘意隨心。只有朋友和家人會期待收到禮物。這個地方的人喜歡收到自己無法輕易取得的東西。例如，阿根廷是主要牛隻和皮革生產國，因此收到皮革製品不會讓他們感到高興。另一方面，酒在阿根廷很昂貴，許多人買不起，因此酒就會是一項不錯的送禮選擇。記得千萬別送黑色或紫色的東西。特別是在巴西，這些顏色是表示哀悼用的。

　　說到送禮，其實重要的是背後的心意。所以下次你送禮物時，請三思而行，以確定你的禮物能傳達出正確的訊息。

解析

1. 本文主要在探討世界各地的送禮文化，何種禮物被視為理想的禮物，以及何種禮物被視為禁忌，故選(A)不同文化之間送適合禮物的概念都不同。

2. 根據第三段第一句的文意：中東各國有自己的送禮「習俗」，也就是(D)廣泛為一般人接受的作法。

3. 根據第四段指出酒在阿根廷很貴，一般人買不起，因而(D)送阿根廷網友酒是適合的禮物。由第二段得知不宜送韓國人尖銳物品，故(A)一把剪刀不合適；由同段知道日本人忌諱數字是四和九的禮物，故(B)四個一組的茶杯不合適；根據第三段知道伊斯蘭教禁止穿金戴絲，故(C)金手鍊不適合。

4. 根據第三段 In Islam, it's important to give and receive gifts with **only the right hand**，可見使用左手是禁忌，故選(C)。

5. 第四段得知在拉丁美洲，只有朋友和家人期待收到禮物，且拉丁美洲人較隨意。可見相較於其他地區，送禮不是很複雜的事情，故選(B)。

---

etiquette　n. 禮節；禮儀　　laid-back　adj. 悠閒的　　mourn　vi./vt. 哀悼

　　「SCUBA (水肺)」這個字其實是縮寫，全名是自攜式水中呼吸裝置，意指潛水者為了抵達海洋深處必須穿戴的一種裝備。一名水肺潛水者需要的基本裝備包括一套能使身體保暖的潛水裝、一件被稱為「浮力調整裝置」的背心、一筒空氣、一條幫助潛水者沈入水中的重量帶、蛙鞋、面罩以及在海面游動時用的呼吸管。其他潛水者可能攜帶的物品包括潛水刀、手電筒、照相機、潛水手套及潛水鞋。

　　海面下的世界讓潛水者有截然不同的體驗，特別是游在波浪底下時那種完全無重力的感覺。除此之外，潛水者呼吸時產生的氣泡聲音是如此有魅力，一旦聽過就永遠不會忘記。世界上每一塊水域都有各自不同的水下環境，每個地方都有新事物可欣賞。一名潛水者可以與海豚共泳、尋找寶藏、為無數美麗魚類拍照和從事其他許多有趣活動。

　　可供潛水者下去潛泳的環境也很多。熱帶島嶼是潛水者最喜歡造訪的地方，雖然沈船和寒冷水域也是潛水者常去之處。從水面到海底，每個環境都是各種不同而奇妙的海中生物之家。不過，在許多地方，海底位於水肺潛水者不可能到達的深處，必須藉由機器才能研究棲息在那的生物。

　　雖然全球海洋平均深度是 13,124 呎，到目前為止水肺潛水的最深紀錄則只達到約 1000 呎，是 2000 年 11 月由一位名叫約翰・班奈特的男子在菲律賓波塞羅拉島附近水域所創下。然而，一般的水肺潛水深度約在 30 到 50 呎之間，使約翰的紀錄無人能及。

　　海浪下有這麼多可供探索的事物，任何人只要穿上一套裝備就可以搖身一變成為探索者。當潛水者在波浪下吸進一口氣，就一定會看到和遇見新鮮事。

1. 第一段提到水肺潛水的裝備，第二段描述水肺潛水的體驗，第三段指出地點重點，故知答案為(B)水肺潛水的一般資訊。(A)(C)(D)只是各段的細節，並非全文主旨。

2. 見第四段 the deepest scuba dive made to date only reached a depth of about **1,000 feet**，故選(C)。

3. 根據第二段 especially a complete **feeling of weightlessness** when one is swimming beneath the waves 故知(D)為答案。(A)為非，由第一段得知 SCUBA 是 Self-Contained Underwater Breathing Apparatus 的縮寫字；(B)為非，見第三段 Tropical islands are the favorite haunt of divers 故不選；(C)為非，見第三段 The bottom of the sea is impossible to reach by scuba divers 故不選。

4. 見第三段 the bottom of the sea is impossible to reach by scuba divers, and machines have to be used to study creatures that live there，故選(A)。(B)為非，與海豚游泳只是浮潛者的樂趣之一，故不選；(C)(D)本文並未提及，故不選。

5. 關鍵字所在的第二段都在敘述浮潛的樂趣，因此可以推論本字的意思是(C)吸引人的。

acronym n. 首字母縮略詞　　apparatus n. 裝置　　fin n. 蛙鞋　　body of water n. 大片的水域
unbeatable adj. 無與倫比的　　gear n. (特種用途的) 衣服，工具　　strap vt. 用帶捆綁

翻譯

　　有很多理由使悲劇一直以來都是劇作家最愛的主題，但其中最重要的是，比起其他訴諸情感為內容的戲劇，悲劇對人類心靈的影響最大。也許這就是為何，許多文學和戲劇中的悲劇英雄往往是全世界觀眾印象最深和最鍾愛的角色。舉例來說，莎士比亞筆下的悲劇英雄如哈姆雷特、馬克白、李爾王以及奧賽羅都是全球著名劇團的劇中主角。這些不折不扣的悲劇，上演次數都比喜劇和通俗劇頻繁許多。

　　有助提升悲劇在戲劇界地位的另一項重要因素是，悲劇幾乎總是在描述顯赫男性和女性的故事。喜劇主要關注一般人的日常生活點滴，悲劇主角則往往是國王、王后和貴族這些理應心智堅強而高尚的人。也許是由於一般大眾心中隱隱抱有看到這些權貴人士犯錯墮落的渴望，因而使悲劇受到廣大歡迎。反過來說，悲劇英雄也為一般民眾提供教訓，讓他們能在生命中避免類似的悲劇發生。例如《李爾王》就告訴我們，若做下錯誤的判斷會有什麼危險，而《哈姆雷特》則細述一名王子如何躊躇猶豫地進行復仇；《奧賽羅》道出嫉妒和缺乏信任的可怕，而《馬克白》則告訴我們空洞的野心是多麼徒勞無用。

　　人們往往會認同自己最喜歡的悲劇英雄，在劇中所見和自己的真實生活經驗之間找到相似之處，因而時常在面對困難情境時得到安慰，並獲得道德勇氣來克服不幸。由是，悲劇協助人們在面臨人生抉擇時做出最好的決定。

解析

1. 第一段第一句就指出有很多原因使悲劇一向是劇作家最喜愛的題材，下面段落提到悲劇受歡迎的原因及分別舉例某些知名悲劇教導大家的道理，故選(C)。

2. 由第二段 tragic characters **provide lessons for ordinary people** to avoid causing tragic situations in their lives 推知答案為(B)。

3. 第二段描述莎翁的悲劇人物馬克白，他的野心最後徒然落空，故(D)馬克白的野心成果豐碩為誤。

4. 第三段中間指出人們將悲劇和自己的生活對照，因此面對困境能夠安慰自己，並有力量克服逆境，這便是受惠於悲劇作品之處，故選(D)。

5. 第三段提到大多數人往往會「認同」自己最喜歡的悲劇英雄。所以可推測關鍵字意同於(A)相似點。

---

endearing adj. 受人喜愛的　　out-and-out adj. 完全的，徹底的　　melodrama n. 通俗劇
protagonist n. 主角　　recount vt. 敘述，講述　　exact vt. 復仇　　futility n. 徒勞，無益

翻譯

　　英國作家拉迪爾・吉卜林曾寫道：「東方是東方，西方是西方，兩者永不該接觸。」當時，西方的人們對亞洲人的生活所知極少，而亞洲對西方亦然。事實上，東西方之間唯一的接觸通常經由貿易，有時則是戰爭。西方曾一度認為東方很奇特、充滿異國情調，也許甚至還有點令人討厭。

　　然而，二十一世紀的現況跟吉卜林的看法正好相反，東方元素激起了西方人的興趣，使他們愛上更多其他東方事物。例如，壽司和泰國食物在西方國家受歡迎的程度直逼披薩和漢堡。在裝潢房子時，有些西方人迷上風水這種中國裝潢藝術概念，藉由安排一個房間的擺設或計畫一棟建築物的方位和設計來確保快樂、平安和富貴。在中國醫學和部分武術中佔有重要地位的無形能量「氣」，則風靡了西方科學家和醫師。有些西方醫院也趕搭上這股熱潮，提供搭配中藥的西式療法。

　　東方對西方的影響已是全世界可見，雙方早已跨越藩籬。越來越多好萊塢名人對中國草藥產生興趣。此外，許多人訴諸針灸來治療疾病或減輕疼痛。對中國武術有興趣的人開始學太極拳，那是一種著重緩慢、冥思動作的古老中國武術；來自印度的瑜珈運動則成為今日的主流運動之一。

　　自從馬可波羅首度將東方引介給西方開始，東方的風格和相關事物就跟西方人產生活躍互動。很明顯地，即使時間漸進，東方流行仍然散播到世界每個角落。

解析

1. 第一段述及東西方缺乏溝通，但隨著第二段的轉折 (However,...) 以及第三段強調西方人對東方文化趨之若鶩的狀況，加上結論 the eastern fashion has spread the length and breath of the world(= to every part of the world) 故選 (C)。

2. 根據第一段 The West once viewed the east as **strange**, **exotic**, and perhaps even a little abominable(=frightful) 句中多個帶有負面涵義的形容詞得知答案為(A)對東方帶有負面看法。

3. 由第二段提到的西方醫院中西藥並用、第三段描述的好萊塢名人中藥熱及針灸療法越來越受歡迎，得知東方對西方最明顯的影響在(B)醫學。

4. 第二段僅提及西方人趕流行中西藥並用，並未強調或證實東方藥物強於西藥，故選(D)。

5. 第二段提及中藥及中國武術所強調的「氣」，讓美國的科學家及醫生對東方文化趨之若鶩的狀況，可以推測此片語意同(C)形成風潮。

---

twain （古英語）二　　abominable adj. 令人討厭的　　whet vt. 刺激，促進
jump on the bandwagon 趕流行；搭上…的熱潮　　resort to 訴諸，求助　　acuncture n. 針灸
relevance n. 關連　　the lenght and breadth of... 遍及…

翻譯

蛇無疑是動物世界中最受厭惡和懼怕的生物之一。由於各種原因，許多人對這種滿身鱗片的動物反感，並讓這種觀念在腦中根深蒂固。根據基督教信仰，蛇是撒旦的使者，因而當受輕視。傳統上，在希臘神話、某些中國神話故事和埃及民間傳說裡，蛇都和惡魔有密切關聯。此外，儘管今日進步的醫療科技，在世界上許多缺少抗蛇毒血清治療的地區，蛇吻仍跟死亡劃上等號。

然而，科學家們指出，在目前所有已知蛇類中，只有不到百分之二十具有毒性。雖然有毒蛇擁有威力強大的毒液，但這些毒液是它們用來使獵物動彈不得和斃命的工具，不過人類並非蛇的天然獵食對象。科學家們相信，蛇其實會特別小心避開人類，而且除非被逼得無路可逃，牠們絕不會正面對上人類。大多數蛇咬人的意外事件都發生在交配和做窩季節，那時牠們的攻擊性最強。我們必須知道，大多數蛇咬人意外都是由於人類侵入牠們的地盤所引起。與蛇和平共處的最佳方式，就是讓蛇留在牠們的自然棲息地。

事實上，蛇是自然食物鏈中非常重要的一環，形成一種能限制齧齒動物和小型哺乳類動物數量的控制機制。牠們控制害蟲數量，是農夫在自然界的朋友。此外還有近期研究顯示，蛇毒有可能減緩一些病症如癌症的加劇速度。世界許多地方都在對蛇毒進行大量研究，以找出它的可能用途。

因此，我們必須瞭解蛇類其實只和其他野生動物一樣危險。如果得到立即而正確的治療，幾乎所有毒蛇咬傷都可以治癒。蛇對人類的益處其實遠大於牠的缺點及對人類的生命威脅，這點豈不令人驚嘆？

解析

1. 雖然第一段提及宗教、傳統以及神話中對於蛇的看法，但第二段開始指出科學家研究顯示有關蛇的事實，故選(C)。
2. 根據第二段末得知多半遭蛇咬意外是因為人類誤闖蛇活動的地盤。所以只要不侵犯牠們，就可相安無事，故選(D)。
3. 第二段中間提及蛇在交配、做窩的季節最具侵犯性，故選(B)。
4. 第三段後半部分指出近來研究顯示蛇的毒液可能減緩某些疾病，如癌症的進展，故選(A)。
5. 第二段第二句提到毒蛇的劇毒是用來 **immobilize** (使無法行動) 並殺死獵物。可見其字義接近(D)使癱瘓。

repulsive adj. 使人反感的　　despise vt. 鄙視　　synonym n. 同義字　　antivenom adj. 抗蛇毒的
potent adj. 有效力的　　trespass vi. 闖入　　mechanism n. 機制　　rodent n. 齧齒動物
outweigh vt. 比⋯更重要

翻譯

　　一項由猶他大學進行的研究提出新證據，顯示駕駛開車時使用手機的分心的程度和酒醉駕車不相上下。有些令人驚訝的是，這項研究也同時發現，即使駕駛使用免持聽筒，分心程度也跟手持電話的駕駛一樣。

　　大衛・史崔爾教授跟他的研究團隊一起和四十名志願者在四種不同模擬狀況下進行這項研究，這些狀況包括專心開車、一邊拿手機講話一邊開車、一邊使用免持聽筒講電話一邊開車，以及酒醉時駕車。研究結果顯示，駕駛不論使用手持或免持電話闖紅燈或發生追撞意外的可能都比專心開車的駕駛大很多。行進中使用手機產品的駕駛人，連清楚辨識視線中物體的能力都會下降。史崔爾教授將這種因講手機而導致的分心狀況稱為「一種因不注意而造成的盲目狀態，會減弱駕駛開車時對重要資訊的警覺。」

　　來自皇家意外事故預防學會的羅傑・文生進一步描述駕駛在行進中使用手機時的行為狀態：「你的注意力會越來越被談話內容吸引住，越放越少在交通狀況上。」他提出有益大眾的作法——開車時不准使用手機的禁令及對違法者的重罰。這項研究再加上先前的其他研究，可能有助於立法禁止駕駛於行進中使用手機產品。「先前許多研究已經指出，開車時如果使用手機，無論是手持或免持式，肇事率都比平常多四倍。」文生如此表示。

　　目前在英國，駕駛人在行進中使用免持手機是合法的。然而，若有證據顯示這些駕駛人無法適當控制自己的車子，他們就有可能被起訴。

解析

1. 本文重點在討論並證明：開車時使用手機是危險的。第二、三段並提出學者的實驗證明及學術報告，故選(D)開車時應禁止使用手持或免持手機。

2. 見第二段：大衛・史崔爾以實驗證明開車時打手機的分心狀況是 a form of inattention blindness, muting drivers' awareness of important information in the driving scene。羅傑・文生在第三段明白指出 a ban on the use of cell phones while driving and tougher penalties for violators，由此可知這兩位學者都反對開車時打手機，故選(B)。

3. 本題考細節，見第三段末...., you are **four times** more likely to crash if you are using a handheld or a hands-free phone，故選(C)。

4. 由第一段 A study...has provided new evidence that the level of distraction experienced by drivers using cell phones is comparable to that experienced by drunk drivers，而第二段接著細述這個實驗，故可知將酒醉駕車包含在實驗內是因為(B)將酒醉駕車與邊打手機邊開車做比較。

5. 由關鍵字後的四種模擬情節可推知是指做實驗時的模擬情境，故選(A)。

handheld　adj. 手持的　　intoxicated　adj. 酒醉的　　rear-end collision　n. 追撞事故　　mute　vt. 減弱
elaborate　vi./vt. 詳盡闡述　　penalty　n. 罰款　　prosecute　vi./vt. 起訴

44 河狸不好惹
Beavers Bite

翻譯

你聽過「忙得像隻河狸一樣」這句話嗎？河狸有可能是自然界最不懈怠的生物，向來以牠們驚人的建築成果聞名。用牙齒啃斷樹來建造水壩阻斷小溪來形成數公尺深的池塘，對牠們來說根本不算什麼。河狸們不會躺在自己的傑作上沾沾自喜，而會接著開始在新弄出的池塘中間用泥土、樹枝和石頭安全地打造出一座小屋。科學家們發現，錄下的水急速流動的聲音會觸發牠們建水壩的本能。

然而，河狸的建築計畫有時會使牠們和人類鄰居產生衝突。當水壩崩塌時，會造成溪水下游地區洪水氾濫。除此之外，因為河狸的水塘越變越大，洪水也會損害溪流的上游地區，淹沒原本乾燥的土地。結果造成樹木和穀物被淹毀。住家、高速公路和鐵路最後也會泡在水裡。人類的水資源被不潔淨的洪水污染，下水道也被樹枝和樹葉阻塞到無法正常運作。

通常的解決辦法是摧毀那些造成問題的水壩，但做起來可不像聽起來那麼容易。河狸們厲害得很，牠們建的是堅固耐久的水壩。有一個破壞方法是以手持工具在水壩上開一個洞，讓水慢慢從洞流乾。要對付較大的水壩，則可能需要重型挖鑿裝置或炸藥才行。這些方式往往會在水壩壞掉時造成下游地區覆滿泥巴、淤泥和水壩殘骸。河狸的小屋通常會在最後被摧毀，因為若摧毀一座小屋卻不摧毀小屋所在的水壩，這樣很難讓河狸家庭搬離。

隨著人類居住地區向外擴張，人們無法不搬入河狸的棲息地，引發一場戰爭。令人難過的是，動物似乎成了輸家。有時候，要跟這些永不倦怠的水壩建造者和平共處，可能意味著必須忍受一些不方便，但只有當河狸的水壩對人類財產造成真正重大威脅時，我們才有理由將它們摧毀。

解析

1. 第一段指出河狸以其神奇的建築工事而聞名。可見用牙齒把樹齧倒築水壩對牠們是稀鬆平常、輕而易舉的事情，故選(A)。
2. 第一段最後指出科學家發現流水聲會引發河狸築壩的本能，故選(D)。
3. 由第二段可知河狸的建築工事所造成的損害。當水塘擴大時，會淹沒上游原來的乾地，故選(B)。
4. 第三段最後指出只破壞河狸的窩而不破壞水壩，這樣不可能讓整窩河狸離開。也就是說要徹底解決問題，就要先破壞水壩，故選(B)。同段指出，用手持工具鑽洞，讓水慢慢漏掉，這是破壞水壩的一種方式，並未如(A)所說的沒有效用；而用重型機械或炸藥破壞水壩會造成淤泥壅塞，但並未顯示嚴重到需要疏散下游居民，故(C)不正確；此外第四段最後指出：唯有當河狸的水壩危及人類的財產時，才需要拆毀它。故不能選(D)不計代價都不容河狸的水壩存在。
5. 根據第四段，作者認為是人類入侵河狸的棲地才會造成兩者間的戰爭，而後者似乎總是處於弱勢。由此可見，作者對河狸是(C)同情。

---

dam n. 水壩　　lodge n. 巢穴　　wipe out 摧毀　　contaminate vt. 弄髒，污染　　silt n. 泥沙
wage vt. 發動 (戰爭)

翻譯

　　還記得那幅如夢般的景象——一隻美人魚坐在一塊美麗的珊瑚礁上納涼，一邊用一片海扇當扇子搧嗎？海扇身為珊瑚家族的一員，其實是由有許多美麗顏色的微小生物或水螅集群所構成。雖然外型看起來像扇子，海扇實際上是一處海中生物居住和覓食的便利家園。

　　海扇最知名的出現地點是溫帶地區如澳洲和紅海，那裡的氣候條件最適合牠們生存，但在寒冷的海域如挪威和阿拉斯加也有牠們的蹤跡。在安全的生存環境下，牠們可以長到幾近兩公尺寬，但卻很容易被大意和魯莽的潛水者或暴風雨弄斷。牠們在絕佳的地點能長成巨大的群落，稱為「海扇森林」。雖然海扇是由硬的物質所構成，但牠們其實會在強的海流中緩緩來回晃動。

　　海扇本身就像一座海底公寓，有許多其他小型植物和動物住在牠們的扇葉裡。包括像極小的海星、蟲子、海綿以及海膽，牠們會稱食物隨波漂過海扇時捕捉它們。我們可以想像一棵由細緻、像蕾絲布邊的珊瑚所形成的扁平狀小樹，它藉由一條粗壯的根和周圍其他珊瑚連接在一起，而這棵小樹往往會朝橫向伸出，攔截一道從暗礁之間狹長隧道流出的海流，使居於其中的動物能更容易捕捉到食物。

　　海扇非常脆弱，很容易被海扇所在的珊瑚礁系統中翻騰的風暴浪折斷。雖然我們無法避免這些自然發生的災害，但我們絕對可以鼓勵人類潛水者和游泳者在游到牠們附近時更謹慎一點。如果能小心謹慎，當我們在珊瑚礁附近游泳或潛水時，必然能永遠欣賞到這些美麗的海扇。

解析

1. 本篇概略地介紹海扇的生長環境；(A)(C)(D)僅提及各段重點，只有(B)海扇的生活狀況涵蓋全文重點。
2. 見第一段 As a member of the **coral family**, sea fans are... 故選(A)。
3. 由第二段 In a protected place they can grow to almost two meters wide, but are easily broken by careless and reckless **divers** or **stormy seas**，故選(D)。
4. 見第二段..., they are also found **in chill sea areas** like Norway and Alaska，故(C)海扇不能在冷水海域生存為錯。
5. 由關鍵字的下一句 With **care**, we should be able to enjoy... 可以推測關鍵字等同於(B)小心的。

chunk　n.　一大塊　　polyp　n.　水螅　　sea urchin　n.　海膽　　lacy　adj.　有花邊的
churn up　劇烈攪動

46 讓腎上腺素狂飆吧
Get the Adrenaline Going

　　水上滑板、高空彈跳以及街頭滑橇這三種極限運動中的寵兒將運動推到極限。極限運動也被稱為動作或冒險運動。比起傳統運動，極限運動牽涉到更多危險性、腎上腺素以及個人成就感，並帶起一類全新的運動族群！

　　極限運動其實就是一些現存運動的危險版。舉例而言，將跳板跳水運動推到極限，就產生了懸崖跳水。如果你在懸崖跳水時錯過正確降落地點，就有可能不是濺起拙劣的水花，而是摔在一堆岩石上跌斷脊椎！極限運動員在進行這些瘋狂運動時，會承受到致命的傷害。世界知名專業極限運動員麥特‧霍夫曼將單車運動推到極限。他因為從事這項運動，已經動過十六次大手術，跌斷超過五十根骨頭。而最嚴重的一次受傷，是發生在他騎著特技單車從23呎高處跳下之後！

　　科學家們相信，極限運動員生來就適合冒這些險。腎上腺素會引起極大的刺激感，驅使這些人做出大多數人幾乎連看都不敢看的特技。他們從事這些危險特技之後腦部所釋放出的化學物質會使他們對這些運動上癮，是他們一次又一次接著嘗試的誘因。對這些運動員而言，高速跳動的心臟和胃裡彷彿在抽筋的感覺，讓這些險都冒得很值得。

　　極限運動吸引一些醉心於個人成就和勝利而非團隊精神的運動員。這些運動中少有規則或裁判，因此運動員需要倚賴創意、技術和大無畏的精神來達成個人的最佳表現。跟傳統運動不一樣的是，這些運動員不太在意獎牌或得名。對他們來說，能達到心理和身體上的目標更重要。在一場賽事之後，年輕粉絲的熱烈支持會驅使這些不怕死的人嘗試更困難的特技。有些時候，真正的好戲那時才開始！

1. 第二段第一句提到極限運動實際上是現有運動的危險版，故選(D)極限運動由現有運動發展而來。此外，由第一段得知 action sports、adventure sports 和 extreme sports 是極限運動的不同名稱，(A)為錯；第四段指出從事極限運動者需要創意、技巧及無畏的勇氣，(B)為錯；由第四段得知，極限運動規則很少，並非沒有規則，(C)為錯。

2. 第二段指出跳板跳水發展到極限成為懸崖跳水。如果落下的位置恰當，應該掉進水裡。但後者一個不小心就會背部著地，落在大岩石上，而非落在水裡濺起一片浪花，故選(D)。

3. 根據第二段，麥特‧霍夫曼使騎自行車變成極限運動，他受傷的紀錄顯示極限運動的「危險性質」，故選(B)。

4. 第三段第一句指出，科學家認為從事極限運動者天生就適合冒險，也就是(A)受到本性的驅使。此外，第四段指出這些人追求個人的成就，不在乎獎牌或得勝。年輕粉絲的興奮情緒會使他們做更大膽、困難的嘗試，故(B)為錯。

5. 關鍵字所在的那句話用(C)激勵、誘因套入，可產生合理句意：「起了激勵作用，使他們一試再試」。

---

adrenaline　n.　腎上腺素　　　luge　n.　仰臥滑行小雪橇　　　breed　n.　種類　　　esprit de corps　團隊精神

翻譯

　　從來沒人見過活生生的大王烏賊。牠們躲在深不見底的黑暗海中,有對足球般大的眼睛,據報牠們還曾經在海中攻擊過鯨魚。雖然牠們很難被找到,我們還是透過老一輩水手講的故事和被沖上各地海灘的龐大屍體,得知牠們就潛藏在海中。

　　史提夫‧歐錫博士是一名動物學家,多年來都在研究這些神秘生物。他經過長久的冒險捕捉到小烏賊後,把牠們放在一個細心控制的人工水底環境中,以便觀察牠們的習性和成長過程。

　　大王烏賊游泳的方式就像水上摩托車,從身體一端將水吸入後,再從另一端以高速噴出。以這種方式,再加上牠們長而薄的身體,使牠們能在水中像魚雷般移動,嚇人又滑溜的觸手則拖在身後。牠們身體其中一端有一張強壯如鳥喙的嘴巴和五對觸手,最薄又最長的一對用來捉住獵物,通常是魚或其他較小的烏賊。一隻大王烏賊每天需要用觸手捕捉許多食物,才能填飽那副巨大的軀體。

　　一般相信,成年的大王烏賊生活在海面下約五百公尺深處。對大多數人來說,這個深度都深到無法以潛水方式抵達。為了研究大王烏賊的棲息地,科學家們必須用上小型潛水艇。

　　不久之前,一具大王烏賊的屍體被沖到紐西蘭南部一處沙灘上。這隻 5.7 公尺長的海中巨物重量超過三百公斤,而且還在一隻海豚的胃裡。這項轟動的發現不久後被運送到歐錫博士位於奧克蘭博物館的實驗室裡。如今,這名海洋生物學權威將能夠解開他對這種海中巨大生物所抱持的一些疑問。

解析

1. 第一段談及大王烏賊的神奇,第二段至末段均是歐錫博士對於大王烏賊的觀察研究,故選(C)。本文並非針對科學家們如何地研究大王烏賊,也未談及其他水中生物,故不選(A)(B),更沒有完全敘述(D)大王烏賊的一生。

2. 見第四段 To study the giant squid's habitat, scientists have to **use small submarines**,故選(D)。

3. 由第三段 The thinnest and longest **pair (of tentacles) is used to catch its prey** 可知答案為(A)。

4. 見第五段 Not long ago, a massive squid **carcass** was found...in southern New Zealand,因 **carcass = dead body** 可知找到的大王烏賊是屍體而非活捉,故知(B)為錯。

5. 見第一段 No one has ever seen a giant squid alive. **Hiding** in the bottomless and dark sea... 及 Though they are **difficult to find** 從以上的句子及畫線部分的線索可以判斷關鍵字意為(B)隱藏。

---

torpedo n.　魚雷　　formidable adj.　令人畏懼的　　slippery adj.　滑的　　tentacle n.　觸手,觸腳
carcass n.　(動物的) 屍體

48 高飛又高薪的工作
The High-flying Job

翻譯

　　一名飛行員的生活從開始進行機上訓練後，就被各種嚴格的要求所掌控。只有很少數的學員能取得完整執照，因為整套訓練需要耗去大量心力和金錢。除了招收學員數量有限之外，多數飛行學校還要求學員須具備大學學歷及無肇事的駕駛記錄。在修習基本知識課程和模擬訓練之餘，許多學員還必須成為飛行教練，才能以經濟上負擔得起的方式取得一般航空公司所要求的一千五百個小時飛行時數。在終於獲得某家航空公司雇用後，飛行員還必須每兩年接受再測試。若沒通過——沒能保有非常好的聽力及視力程度——就會失去已取得的飛行執照。

　　一名飛行員肩負的責任比一般朝九晚五的上班族大許多，因為他必須為機上所有乘客和機組人員的性命負責。飛機上每一個人都信任飛行員能安全而及時地起飛和降落。惡劣天候、系統失靈以及安全漏洞等，還只是一名飛行員必須臨機處理的許多主要問題中的幾項而已。除了緊要的不包括在飛行時間內需盡的義務，如平衡行李艙重量和記錄飛航日誌以外，飛行員還得為一架價值五、六千萬美元的飛機負責，而且還不是他的！

　　飛行員的工作班表幾乎比其他任何職業都來得嚴苛。一般飛行員普遍依排班制工作，連續工作許多天再連休幾天更是常有的事，此外許多休假還得在遠離家鄉的不佳地點排遣。另一方面，資深飛行員的選擇權較大，可以選擇想飛的航線，也往往可將休假安排在溫暖的度假地點度過。不幸的是，飛行員得在飛行許多年後才能享受這些額外好處，而且還無法持續多久，因為在大多數國家，飛行員在六十歲之前就被要求要退休了。

解析

1. 本文各段分別提及民航機飛行員所需具備的條件、要擔負的責任及特殊的工作時間，所以是讓讀者對這們行業有較深入的認識，故選(C)。

2. 第一段提到多數訓練飛行員的學校要求具備大學學位以及開車無肇事記錄，不過這並不等於所有航空公司設定的條件，故選(C)。

3. 根據第二段，(A)處理劫機事件、(B)檢查飛行高度表、(C)注意路線內天氣狀況應包含在飛行員所擔負的責任中。此外，文章提到要調整行李艙裡旅客的行李以保持平衡，而非(D)徹底檢查旅客的護照。

4. 根據文章看來，民航機飛行員需符合嚴格的要求才能具備資格，飛行時承擔重大責任、工作時間不固定，符合(A)必須承受身心壓力。文章最後提到，飛行員規定六十歲前退休，而年資夠久才能享受福利，因此享有福利的時間其實很短暫 (short-lived)。所以(B)飛行員壽命較短非正確。至於(C)擔任飛行教練賺取額外收入能讓飛行員過奢華的生活亦非正解。因為文章第一段只提到很多學員必須擔任飛行教練，才能負擔 1,500 小時飛行時間的費用。

5. 關鍵字出現在「選擇飛行路線」、「安排在溫暖的終點站渡假」之後，可見這是指資深飛行員享受的(B)福利。

---

twenty-twenty adj. 視力正常的　　　nine-to-five adj. 上班時間朝九晚五的　　　promptly adv. 準時地
breach n. 缺口　　　logbook n. 航空日誌

翻譯

「唉呀！」這是當事情不如預期且出錯時，查理布朗這個角色會咕噥著說出的名言。

查理布朗是漫畫家查爾斯‧舒茲的連環漫畫《史努比》裡眾多原創角色之一。雖然這部連環漫畫在 1950 年首度開始連載時，查理布朗這個角色比較自以為是而愛惡作劇，但他很快就變成如今我們所熟知的可愛失敗者。舒茲以自己的生活為靈感，將查理布朗塑造成一個害羞的男孩，他對世界有一套獨特看法，很容易擔心，令其他人老想去嘲諷他，佔他便宜。

在這部漫畫連載的五十年間，這名穿黃色襯衫的男孩經常失敗。每年秋天他都試圖踢出美式足球季的第一個好球，但每一次，他那位似乎很喜歡看他掙扎的鄰居露西，都在他的腳正要碰到球那一刻把球抽走。每次他想帶領他的小聯盟棒球隊獲得冠軍，都會以失敗收場，只得到兩勝九百三十敗的戰績。

要把查理布朗想成一個可悲的角色很容易。他的朋友們叫他「笨瓜」，說他是個「平淡無味」的傢伙。即使他的狗史奴比都不屑地說他是「那個頭圓圓的小子」。查理布朗自己認為他的生命實在不怎麼樣。他曾在漫畫裡說過：「有時候我半夜躺在床上睡不著，問自己：『我到底做錯了什麼？』接著有個聲音對我說：『那一個晚上也說不完。』」

看來，似乎這個頭上無毛的小孩從來沒做對半件事，但這麼想可就錯了。查理布朗想戰勝困境的決心、他對別人的體貼，甚至他每次以有風度的方式面對自己的失敗，都使他成為受到粉絲喜愛和尊敬的角色。畢竟，還有什麼比一個即使每件事似乎都在唱反調卻仍然拒絕投降的人更適合當我們的模範呢？

解析

1. 本文敘述查理布朗如何被創造出來，以及他受讀者歡迎的原因，故選(C)查理布朗及他對讀者的影響。其他三個選項只是各段的重點，並未涵蓋全篇。

2. 由第二段 Using his own life as inspiration, Schulz molded Charlie Brown...，故知答案為(D)。

3. 由第二段 Although Charlie Brown... 一句中的 assertive 和 mischievous 而知答案為(A)。

4. 根據第五段 Charlie Brown's determination to triumph... 一句得知(B)為錯，查理布朗靠的是決心、體貼、面對失敗的風度贏得讀者的心，而非他的幽默。

5. 由關鍵字前句中所包含的 pathetic (=sad) character、blockhead (=a stupid person) 一連串負面的形容詞可推斷關鍵字亦屬負面字眼；四個選項中，只有(D)優柔寡斷屬負面字眼，故為答案。

---

catchphrase n. 名言　　mutter vi./vt. 咕噥，低聲嘀咕　　assertive adj. 肯定的

mischievous adj. 惡作劇的，調皮的　　pathetic adj. 可憐的　　blockhead n. 傻瓜，笨蛋　　tot n. 小孩

翻譯

你曾想過要當一個雜技表演者、特技表演者或馴獸師嗎？對世界各地許多娛樂表演者來說，得到這些在馬戲團裡帶給人歡樂的工作是他們的夢想。然而，要讓這個夢想成真，意味著你得更努力工作而非玩樂。

就像大多數工作一樣，應徵馬戲團職缺是一項競爭的過程。馬戲團表演者雖然來自各種生活背景，但許多人都在體操、舞蹈或劇場表演方面擁有深厚的底子。因此，馬戲界的菜鳥很難打敗那些馬戲團的料得到工作。

馬戲團表演者必須比幾乎所有其他職業的人都加倍努力工作。並不是光穿上一套炫麗服裝，就能讓你每天都找出足以進行訓練、排演以及表演的能量。馬戲團表演者不只要每天都衝勁十足，同時也必須好好照顧自己。馬戲團裡不容許出錯。從小丑到大膽的走鋼索者，全都必須表現完美。

加入馬戲團也表示你得接受一種不斷旅行的生活方式。除了一次得離家幾個月之久，把異鄉或是住滿許多表演者的擁擠拖車當成家在這行是家常便飯。當馬戲團開始演出時，表演者可能一週七天都要工作，包括假日在內。

不像在法律事務所或醫生診所的工作，馬戲團工作並沒有保障。可能馬戲團經營不下去，表演者們就必須找新的馬戲團工作，一切又得從頭開始。嘗試應徵新工作和交新朋友都是一些必經過程。

隨著一些馬戲團如太陽劇團的成功，馬戲團也受到歡迎，越來越多人夢想能在馬戲團內工作。馬戲團的光鮮亮麗只是舞台上營造出來的假象。然而，若馬戲團工作真是你的天職，你會忍受所有困境，換得夜復一夜聽見觀眾瘋狂叫好的機會。

解析

1. 文章首尾兩段都指出馬戲團的表演生涯不是表面那般絢爛，令人欣羨，其實是苦多於樂的，故選(A)馬戲團的生活其實比眼前見到的還多。

2. 最後一段指出太陽馬戲團表演成功，故選(D)。片語 full of beans 意為體力充沛，並非指豆子是馬戲團內帶來好運的象徵，故(A)為錯；第二段指出新手想跟深具體操、舞蹈、戲劇經驗的老手競爭，進入馬戲團的機會很渺茫，故(B)馬戲團提供新手和老手相同的機會為錯；第五段指出馬戲團無法保證提供穩定的工作，故(C)為錯。

3. 第三段提及馬戲團表演者要能吃苦、天天要體力充沛，要好好照顧自己，表演要完美、不能出錯，而且要適應巡迴各地表演、到處為家的生活，故(C)不願巡演各國和睡在拖車的雜技表演者不適任馬戲團的工作。

4. 文章各段都指出馬戲團這行業，不但競爭激烈，工作辛苦而且不穩定。但是最後一段提到，如果你天生適合吃這行飯，你就可以享受觀眾的喝采。綜觀全文，只有客觀分析，而無主觀的好惡，故選(B)。

5. 文章最後一段提到越來越多人夢想「進入馬戲團這個行業」，因而關鍵字指的就是(B)馬戲團在裡面表演的大帳篷。

---

juggler n. 雜技表演者　　audition vi. 試鏡；試演　　all walks of life 各行各業　　outperform vt. 勝過
full of beans 精神飽滿　　audacious adj. 大膽的　　Cirque du Soleil 太陽劇團　　calling n. 職業；天職

透過閱讀，你我得以跨越時空，一窺那已無法觸及的世界

閱讀經典文學時光之旅：英國篇
宋美瑾　編著

閱讀經典文學時光之旅：美國篇
陳彰範　編著

- 各書精選8篇經典英美文學作品，囊括各類議題，如性別平等、人權、海洋教育等。獨家收錄故事背景知識補充，帶領讀者深入領略經典文學之美。
- 附精闢賞析、文章中譯及電子朗讀音檔，自學也能輕鬆讀懂文學作品。
- 可搭配新課綱加深加廣選修課程「英文閱讀與寫作」及多元選修課程。

20分鐘稱霸大考英文作文

王靖賢　編著

- 共16回作文練習，涵蓋大考作文3大題型：看圖寫作、主題寫作、信函寫作。根據近年大考趨勢精心出題，題型多元且擬真度高。
- 每回作文練習皆有為考生精選的英文名言佳句，增強考生備考戰力。
- 附方便攜帶的解析本，針對每回作文題目提供寫作架構圖，讓寫作脈絡一目了然，並提供範文、寫作要點、寫作撇步及好用詞彙，一本在手即可增強英文作文能力。

關於Reading Power

這是一套為愉悅英語而生，

一套能體驗英閱樂趣，

進階閱讀攻略　精采內容

★ 文章題材多元有趣，內容字字珠璣，段落條理分明，並符合大考中心公布之
字表範圍，讓你增廣見聞、提高閱讀能力。

★ 出題方向確實掌握閱讀測驗的基本五大題型，讓你面對各種考試皆能得心應
手、百戰百勝。

★ 翻譯與解析內容詳盡，包括文章翻譯、試題說明和難字整理，提供有效率的
學習模式，並幫助你達到自我評量的最佳效果。

一套能開拓視野見聞，

一套能厚植英語實力，

一套讓人愛不釋手的系列叢書。

「進階閱讀攻略」與
「翻譯與解析」不分售
95-80736G

三民網路書店
www.sanmin.com.tw